SPURGEON

Heir of the Puritans

Ernest W. Bacon

Arlington Heights, Illinois

Christian Liberty Press

1996

Reprinted with permission in 1996 by

Christian Liberty Press

502 West Euclid Avenue

Arlington Heights, Illinois 60004

Book designed by Eric D. Bristley

Set in Minion

Printed in the United States of America

We would like to thank Dr. Robert Rodgers for the use of his original manuscripts of Spurgeon's sermons.

Preface

Spurgeon was steeped in and fashioned by the writings and principles of the Puritans, and can only be understood in their light. This book, therefore, makes no apology for presenting him as "heir of the Puritans." Both in his preaching of Christ, in his controversies, and in his personal life, he would not have been what he was without them.

In the Sermons there are embedded many autobiographical glimpses of the Prince of Preachers, and I have garnered not a few for this book. I was brought up in the Spurgeon tradition. My parents knew Spurgeon well, and were often at his house in their younger days. Many were the stories about him told in our family. One of the earliest things I remember is the picture of the great preacher hanging on the wall, with many small portraits surrounding it within the same frame—the Metropolitan Tabernacle, the Stockwell Orphanage, the pulpit of New Park Street strangely placed in a tree, probably in his garden, etc. Another of my early memories is of a phrase used concerning the great man—"An ugly man made beautiful by the grace of God." I wondered in my childish way what this thing called "grace" could be which could make such a transformation. Years later, I am thankful to say, I knew.

Wherever possible I have tried to let Spurgeon himself speak, in the events of his life, and in his theological beliefs. Indented quotations are mostly taken from his *Autobiography* or the Sermons.

For nearly forty years I have read the works of the Puritans—if not as deeply as Spurgeon did, at least with as great a love. Like him, also, I have an especial love for Thomas Brooks. I would here like to acknowledge my deep debt to Dr. Alexander Whyte, himself a great lover of Spurgeon, who first inspired me to seek out and read the Puritans for myself. The quotations from the Puritan writers which head each chapter have been chosen with great care, and the reader is urged to read these great men of God for himself.

Some paragraphs from chapter 10 have been taken from an article on "The Puritans and their Preaching" contributed to *The Gospel Magazine.* I have to thank the following for helpful suggestions and the loan of books: Dr. L. G. Champion, Principal of Bristol Baptist College, my friend and fellow student; Mr. Cecil Grubb; Mr. Percy H. R. Hide, Secretary of Spurgeon's Homes; Dr. E. K. H. Jordan; the Rev. Malcolm Pollock MA; and the Rev. L. P. Willmer, a good friend who many years ago gave me a number of complete sets of the Puritan writers, thereby greatly enriching my spiritual understanding. To all these friends I extend my sincere gratitude.

I must also express my very great gratitude to Dr. D. Martyn Lloyd-Jones, an authority on the Puritan era and a great lover of Spurgeon, for so kindly reading this book. My own debt to him for his clear and vital teaching is tremendous, and I am greatly honored that, as Chairman of the "Puritan and Reformed Studies Conference," he should so willingly and warmly commend this new study of a great man of God and the source from which he drew his strength.

May the blessing of God rest upon this book.

—ERNEST W. BACON

Contents

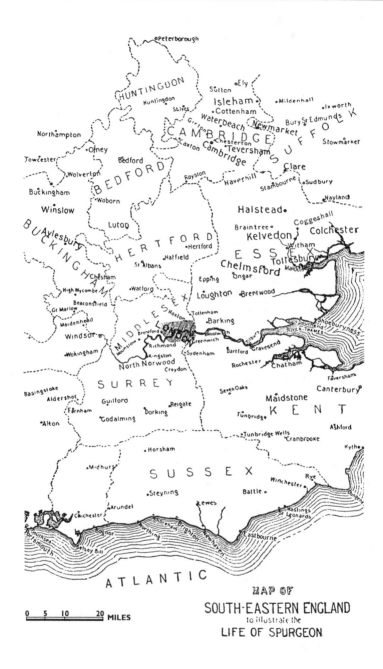

MAP OF
SOUTH-EASTERN ENGLAND
to illustrate the
LIFE OF SPURGEON

CHRONOLOGY OF THE LIFE OF CHARLES SPURGEON

1834	Born at Kelvedon, Essex, June 19.
1835	With grandparents at Stambourne, Essex, August.
1841	Returns to parental home at Colchester, August.
1849	School at Newmarket, August.
1850	Conversion at Colchester, January 6.
	Baptized at Islesham Ferry, May 3.
	Usher at Leeding's School, Cambridge, June 20.
	Joins St. Andrew's Street Baptist Church, Cambridge, October 2.
1851	First sermon at Teversham, Cambs, Spring.
1852	Student-Pastor of Waterbeach Baptist Chapel, January 1852 to February 1854.
1853	First sermon at New Park Street Baptist Chapel, London, December 18.
1854	Commences ministry at New Park Street, March.
1855	Preaches in Exeter Hall, February-March.
1856	Married to Susannah Thompson, January 8.
	Twin sons born, September 20.
	Surrey Music Hall tragedy, October 19.
	Morning services, Surrey Music Hall, November 1856 to December 1859.
1857	Preaches to over 20,000 at Crystal Palace, October 7.
1859	Foundation stone of the Metropolitan Tabernacle laid on August 16.
1861	The Metropolitan Tabernacle opened, March 25.
1864	The "Baptismal Regeneration" Controversy.
1867	Foundation stone of Stockwell Orphanage laid, August 9.
1869	"Helensburgh," Clapham, built, Summer.
1874	Twin sons baptized, September 21.
1880	Moves to "Westwood," Upper Norwood, Summer.
1887	The "Down-Grade" Controversy, 1887-1889.
1891	Last sermon in the Tabernacle, June 7.
1892	Died at Mentone, January 31.
	Buried at West Norwood, February 11.

Spurgeon's Birthplace

Chapter 1
Early Years

Children are their parents' heirs; the mercies of God are not the least part of the parents' treasure, nor the least of the children's inheritance, being helps for their faith, matter for their praise, and spurs to their obedience.

—WILLIAM GURNALL, *THE CHRISTIAN IN COMPLETE ARMOUR*

Charles Haddon Spurgeon was born on June 19, 1834, in a picturesque little cottage at Kelvedon, Essex, still a pleasant rural country town. He belonged to a sturdy lower middle class family which had been strongly Nonconformist[1] for generations. It is on record that one of his ancestors, Job Spurgeon, in the seventeenth century, was imprisoned for attending a Nonconformist meeting. Some of Spurgeon's biographers have urged that his ancestors were probably Dutch refugees who fled to England in 1568 from the persecution of Protestants under the Duke of Alva. It may have been so, for the great preacher was of conventional Dutch build, and through the passing centuries the family could have had an admixture of Dutch blood. On the other hand, some of his biographers urge that his ancestors were Norsemen, and that the name Spurgeon was derived from the Norse word *sporr*, a sparrow. Still others suggest that the Spurgeon family is of French Huguenot[2] origin.

---

1. Protestants in England who refused to become members of the Anglican Church. Also known as *Dissenters*—those who refused to accept the doctrines and forms of the Established Church in England and Scotland.

2. French Reformed Protestants of the sixteenth and seventeeenth centuries.

His father, John Spurgeon, then aged twenty-four, was a clerk in a coal yard, and also the honorary pastor of the Independent (or Congregational) Church at Tollesbury. Here for sixteen years he preached the evangelical Calvinist doctrines to a warm-hearted and loyal congregation. Later he was pastor of the church at Cranbrook, and later still he ministered at Fetter Lane, London, and Upper Street, Islington. He died in 1902, having lived to see his son become the most famous preacher of his day.

His mother, Eliza Jarvis, was barely nineteen when Charles, her eldest child, was born. According to James A. Spurgeon, her second son, she was "the starting point of all greatness and goodness that any of us, by the grace of God, have enjoyed." Altogether seventeen children were born to her, nine of whom died in infancy (as was too often the sad experience of those days), two boys and six girls surviving. Charles always held her in special reverence, and many were the tender and spiritual letters she received from him.

Ten months after his birth, his parents moved to Colchester, and within eighteen months—"on account of unfavorable circumstances"—the baby was sent to live with his grandparents, the Rev. and Mrs. James Spurgeon, in the large manse of the Independent Chapel at Stambourne. Probably the unfavorable circumstances had to do with bad housing, but for whatever reason the next six years of his life, impressionable, formative years for all at that age, were spent under the care of his grandparents and his maiden aunt, Ann Spurgeon. Splendidly did they fulfill their loving responsibility, and Charles always retained a warm affection for them.

We do well to take notice of this family of three into whose care Charles came. The Rev. James Spurgeon, born in 1776, became Pastor at Stambourne in 1810, and ministered at the Meeting-House there for no less a period than fifty-four years, until his death in 1864. Although a man of the old, thorough going Calvinist school, he was a man of wide sympathies and

Rev. James Spurgeon

a notable preacher of the Gospel. He wore the knee-breeches, buckled shoes and silk stockings of the reign of George the Third, a picture of neatness and a lover of young people. In the years to come he was to delight in Charles's success as a warrior of the Lord.

The Old Manse and Meeting-House at Stambourne

The grandmother was a sweet and loving soul. Her piety and useful labors, it is recorded, made her a valuable helpmeet to her husband in every good work. Charles long remembered her with her open Bible sitting by the great fireplace and speaking of the love of God. One Sunday morning in the eventide of this devoted couple, she remarked to her old husband that she did not feel well, and would stay at home and read her Bible and pray, while he preached. On his return he found her in the old armchair, her Bible spread out on her lap, her spectacles across it, her head bowed upon her breast, still in death. Her finger was resting upon Job 19:21—"The hand of God hath touched me!"

Ann Spurgeon, the unmarried daughter of the household, was seventeen when Charles came to them. She was, by all accounts, a radiant young girl of a lovely spirit, and she came to have chief charge of the newcomer. She taught him his letters (she was proud of this later on!), and she encouraged in him that irresistible gift of fun that was so marked in his character in later years.

The little village of Stambourne nestled near the source of the Colne River, a pleasant, peaceful place with its farms, cottages and blacksmith's shop. The Manse at Stambourne was an old, roomy two-storied house. It had a brick hall floor, sprinkled with sand which was kept in a cupboard under the stairs. Its windows were in part plastered, in order to escape the window tax of those days. In one of its attics Charles discovered a large number of books, amongst which was an old copy of Bunyan's *Pilgrim's Progress*, illustrated with amazing woodcuts. He promptly carried it downstairs and began to read. It was as the opening of a new world to him. Bunyan's masterpiece became one of his favorite books, which he claimed to have read over one hundred times. Thus it will be seen that his introduction to Puritan writers, to whom he owed such a deep debt, began before he was six years old!

John Bunyan, the Puritan

Sunday by Sunday the little lad watched his grandfather ascend the steep stairs of the Independent Chapel pulpit, and listened as he poured out a flood of eloquence concerning Christ and His grace freely given to sinners. He probably understood but little, and yet all unconsciously he was being impressed by the fact that a pulpit was a throne, and a Gospel preacher was one of the most important men in the world.

In August 1841 Charles, aged seven, returned to his parents' home at Colchester. It was a deep sorrow for him to leave his grandfather and grandmother and Aunt Ann. But the minister comforted his grandson by telling him that when he looked up at the shining moon at Colchester he must remember that it was the same moon his grandfather would see at Stambourne. For years the boy never saw the moon without thinking of his grandfather. He was not to be cut off from his beloved friends at Stambourne. Year by year he would visit them for holidays, and he kept in touch with them all their days.

At Colchester, Charles found two sisters and a brother, and quickly became their leader. In his *Autobiography* he speaks lovingly of his mother's influence upon them.

> I have not the powers of speech to set forth my valuation of the choice blessing which the Lord bestowed on me in making me the son of one who prayed for me and prayed with me. How can I ever forget when she bowed her knee, and with her arms about my neck, prayed: "O that my son might live before Thee!"

He goes on to record that on Sunday evenings, instead of going to service, mother and children sat round the table, and as they each read the Bible in turn, she would explain the passage, verse by verse, and then pray for them. Afterwards she would read a passage or two from Richard Alleine's *Alarm to the Unconverted*, or Richard Baxter's *Call to the Unconverted*, and press the points home to her children.

A recent writer has spoken of the "years of mental and spiritual torture" in Spurgeon's youth, and adds: "One cannot help feeling that his godly parents contributed to this in no small measure, as they held before his childish mind the terrors of the damned, and earnestly besought him to flee from the wrath to come." There is, of course, absolutely no evidence that Spurgeon as a child was subjected to anything of the kind. On the contrary, the atmosphere of his early home was good, kind and loving, not at all severe, and his parents wisely and gently sought to form his mind and character on the Gospel of the love of Christ.

Spurgeon attended, first of all, a dame school kept by a Mrs. Cook, and later on a school presided over by Mr. Henry Lewis. Here, at the age of ten, he gained the first class English prize, a copy of White's *Natural History of Selborne*, a book he much treasured. At fourteen, Charles and his brother James were sent to Maidstone as pupils at All Saints' Agricultural College, not with the idea of training them to be farmers, but because an uncle was one of the tutors there. Here Charles made steady progress in all subjects, especially in arithmetic, pointing out a mathematical mistake of his uncle's with great glee.

During these early days his passion for reading continued unabated. His father's collection of books included many volumes of the works of the Puritans, and young Spurgeon delved into them eagerly. He read among others Baxter's *Call to the Unconverted*, James's *Anxious Enquirer*, Foxe's *Book of Martyrs*, Doddridge's *Rise and Progress of Religion in the Soul*, and Scougal's *The Life of God in the Soul of Man*. For lighter reading there was Defoe's *Robinson Crusoe*, Shakespeare's plays, and the poems of John Milton and William Cowper (He delighted in *The Task* and also the moral satires of Cowper.) Heavy fare, some will think, for a boy of his age. Many men of mature intellect find such books heavy going. But Charles was a bright lad, and was nourished both mentally and spiritually by them.

We may conclude this part of our narrative by looking at the world of 1834 into which Spurgeon was born. William the Fourth, "the sailor king," was on the throne. Lord Grey, Lord Melbourne, and the great Duke of Wellington were successively prime ministers. Queen Victoria came to the throne in 1837. The first Reform Bill had been passed by a Whig Government in 1832. Trade unions were beginning to be organized, but the poverty of the lower wage earners was great and distressing. In the cotton factories of Lancashire the average weekly wage was nine shillings and ninepence; Yorkshire woolen weavers earned twenty shillings; a builder's laborer in London might earn eighteen shillings; agricultural wages varied in different parts of the country, from seven shillings per week in Wiltshire and Suffolk, to twelve shillings per week in Yorkshire. Unemployment was rife, and in 1842 paupers numbered no less than 1,427,187.

In religion the Church of England was dominant and largely under the influence of a latitudinarian[3] liberalism with no message of salvation or hope for the people. According to Mr. Dean Church, the country parson was "a country gentleman in orders, who rode to hounds and shot and danced and farmed, and often did worse things." He was also very often a pluralist,[4] and generally unpopular. At the same time Evangelicals[5] in the Established Church [of England and Scotland], like Charles Simeon of Cambridge, were making their influence felt, and seeking to secure the appointment of those who preached the Gospel to parish livings. 1833 saw the rise of the Tractarians,[6] and the increasing spread and dominance of the High Church[7] and Sacerdotal party,[8] some of whom were to follow Newman to Rome.

The Nonconformists were a formidable religious force in the life of the nation, although by this time the impulse of the Evangelical Revival had slackened amongst them. Their strength was in the middle and working classes, and in the large towns. Robert Hall, the famous preacher, had died in 1831, but there were other giants left like Thomas Binney, Dr. Rippon, Dr. Baldwin Brown, John Angell James, Josiah Conder, J. H. Hinton, Dr. James Bennett, Dr. F. A. Fox and Dr. Thomas Price. The Nonconformists, however, still suffered from various civil disabilities, and were not admitted to the universities until 1870.

In spite of the deadness amongst many of the churches, they were days in which God was believed in, Sunday strictly kept, and the Scrip-

---

3. A kind of religious liberalism that cares little about particular creeds and forms.

4. A person who believes that ultimate reality has more than one true explanation. The country parson often did not hold to the Reformation doctrine of *Sola Scriptura* (Scripture alone), which states that the Bible is the only source of knowledge regarding God and man and, therefore, the sole means by which ultimate reality can be explained.

5. Those Protestants which emphasize salvation by faith alone (*Sola Fide*) in the atonement of Jesus Christ, and reject the Roman Catholic doctrine that the power of the sacraments and good works are effective in securing one's salvation. Also the Low Church party within the Church of England; this party is strongly evangelical.

6. Also known as the Oxford Movement, which placed the authority of the church over the Bible. Many of this sect later were welcomed into the Roman Catholic Church.

7. A party within the Church of England which emphasizes the importance of the priesthood and the traditional rituals and doctrines.

8. A party within the Church of England which believes in the divine authority of the priesthood.

tures honored and read.

Charles Lamb died in 1834, the year of Spurgeon's birth, and so did Samuel Taylor Coleridge. Wordsworth was still alive but not writing very much now. On the other hand, young Alfred Tennyson was busy polishing his verses, sure that one day he would astonish the world. A young man named Charles Dickens was a hard worked Parliamentary shorthand writer, his fame before him. Down at Plymouth, J. N. Darby was beginning his labors among "The Brethren." Thomas Arnold was the vigorous headmaster of Rugby, bent on revolutionizing the public school system. And far from our shores, Charles Darwin, naturalist of the survey ship *Beagle,* was laying the foundation of his scientific knowledge and pondering his subsequently formulated theory of evolution, or natural selection, which was to shake the scientific and theological worlds to their foundations.

Slavery was abolished throughout the British Empire in 1834, the slave-owners being compensated to the extent of twenty million pounds, which many public spirited and humanitarian citizens thought altogether wrong. In Spain the Carlist[9] civil war was in full swing, and in France Republican insurrections were already breaking out. South Australia was colonized in that year, and Thomas, son of Charles Haddon Spurgeon, was to preach the Gospel there in years to come. There was feverish building of railways throughout the country, and even more feverish financial speculation in railway shares, in which fortunes were made and lost almost overnight. On the other hand, no public libraries existed before 1845, and the percentage of illiterates in 1839 was 41.6 per cent. Sadly, few churchmen at this time saw the need to establish Christian schools to help deal with the illiteracy problem.

Such was the world into which Spurgeon was born, a world vastly different from our own. Yet man's basic needs, material, moral, and spiritual in essence, were the same as ours today. And in the fullness of the time, and in the purpose of God, He sent Charles Haddon Spurgeon to preach the Everlasting Gospel, and to prepare men for Himself.

---

9. This political conflict was instigated by Don Carlos (1788-1855), who claimed to be the rightful successor to the Spanish throne.

Chapter 2
Into the Light

It is profitable for Christians to be often calling to mind the Beginnings of Grace within their Souls.

—JOHN BUNYAN, *GRACE ABOUNDING*

Regeneration is a universal change of the whole man. It is a new creature, not only a new power or new faculty. It extends to every part; understanding, will, conscience, affections, all were corrupted by sin, all are renewed by grace. Grace sets up its ensigns in all parts of the soul, surveys every corner, and triumphs over every lurking enemy; it is as large in renewing as sin was in defacing. The whole soul shall be glorified in heaven; therefore the whole soul shall be beautified by grace.

—STEPHEN CHARNOCK, *THE NATURE OF REGENERATION*

Many and varied are the God-blessed influences that lead to the conversion of a soul. In Spurgeon's case a deep impression was made on him when, a lad of ten, he was on holiday at his grandfather's parsonage at Stambourne. In the summer of 1844 the Rev. Richard Knill came to stay at this house on missionary deputation for the London Missionary Society. He was minister of Queen Street Congregational Church, Chester, where his portrait still hangs, with these words under it: "Brethren, the heathen are perishing. Shall we let them perish? God forbid!" He had spent some years in India in the service of the Gospel, but had been sent back home due to illness. He was also a prolific tract writer; some fourteen million of his tracts having been circulated.

Mr. Knill was greatly drawn to Charles, and during his three days' stay at Stambourne attached himself to the boy as often as possible. In the early mornings he took him into the garden, and there in a yew tree arbor spoke to him of the love of Christ, and prayed with him. On his last morning, in the presence of the family, he took Charles on his knee and uttered a remarkable prophecy: "This child will one day preach the Gospel, and he will preach it to great multitudes. I am persuaded that he will preach in the chapel of Rowland Hill." He also made the boy promise to learn Cowper's hymn, "God moves in a mysterious way His wonders to perform," and to see that it was sung when he preached in Rowland Hill's chapel. Charles solemnly promised. Rowland Hill, a stalwart of Nonconformity, exercised a powerful ministry at Surrey Chapel in London, where great crowds gathered to hear him. Years later, when a famous preacher himself, Charles Haddon Spurgeon preached in Rowland Hill's pulpit and, filled with emotion, told the story of his boyhood and Mr. Knill's prophecy. "To me," he declared, "it was a very wonderful thing, and I no more understood at that time how it could come to pass than I understand today why the Lord should be so gracious to me." Cowper's hymn was sung.

In the autumn of 1849 Charles, aged fifteen, went to Newmarket, Cambridgeshire, to the school of Mr. John Swindell. Here he was an *usher*, the old phrase for an assistant teacher, and made good progress in his studies of Greek, Latin, and philosophy, as well as helping in the teaching of the younger children. In the school debates he astonished his hearers by the agility of his mind and his grasp of the essential points of any argument.

But what of his religious life? For some considerable time, it would seem, he was under strong spiritual stress. The Spirit was stirring him in his quest for a real knowledge of God and salvation. The sermons he heard, the Puritan authors he was reading—like Goodwin's *The Object and Acts of Justifying Faith*—made a deep impression on him, and planted in him the deep desire for a first-hand knowledge of the truth of the Gospel in personal experience. Sin was a reality; he longed for Christ and His grace to be a reality also. Long afterwards he wrote:

> Let none despise the stirrings of the Spirit in the hearts of the young, let not boyish anxieties and juvenile repentances be lightly regarded. I, at least, can bear my personal testimony to the fact that grace operates on some minds at a period almost too early for recollection. When but

Thomas Goodwin

young in years I felt much sorrow for sin. Day and night God's hand was heavy on me. If I slept at night I dreamed of the bottomless pit, and when I awoke I seemed to feel the misery I had dreamed. Up to God's house I went; my song was but a sigh. To my chamber I retired, and there, with tears and groans, I offered up my prayer without a hope and without a refuge, for God's law was flogging me with its two-thonged whip, and then rubbing me with brine afterwards, so that I did shake and quiver with pain and anguish.

It was my sad lot to feel the greatness of my sin without a discovery of the greatness of God's mercy. I had to walk through this world with more than a world upon my shoulders, and I wonder to this day how it was that my hand was kept from rending my own body in pieces through the awful agony which I felt when I discovered the greatness of my transgression. I used to say, "If God does not send me to hell, He ought to do it." I sat in judgment upon myself and pronounced the sentence that I felt would be just. I could not have gone to heaven with my sin unpardoned, even if I had the offer to do it, for I justified God in my own conscience, while I condemned myself.

The Law had truly entered into his conscience with convicting power, that it might act as "a schoolmaster to lead him to Christ." Yet he seemed no nearer an experience of saving grace. "Yet the simplest of all matters—believing in Christ crucified, accepting His finished salvation, being nothing and letting Him be everything, doing nothing but trusting to what He has done—I could not get hold of it."

When I was in the hands of the Holy Spirit under conviction of sin, I had a clear and sharp sense of the justice of God. Sin, whatever it might be to other people, became to me an intolerable burden. It was not so much that I feared hell as that I feared sin; and all the while I had upon my mind a deep concern for the honor of God's name, and the integrity of His moral government. I felt that it would not satisfy my conscience if I could be forgiven unjustly.

Pondering this, we may well consider whether in our modern age, and with our modern evangelism, that we have not stressed enough the fact of sin, the transgression of God's Law, and the necessity for repentance as well as faith. A cheap and superficial solution to the moral ills of man will produce shallow and unstable believers. We are in danger of trying to heal the moral and spiritual hurt of man slightly. Appeals to people to "decide for Christ," without making them thoroughly aware of their sins, and God's judgment on their sins, and without calling for real repentance, is not the Gospel preaching of the New Testament. The "law-work" in the soul, pressed home by the Puritans and by Whitefield and Edwards, produced deep and convinced believers.

Sometimes the young Spurgeon was under the grip of blasphemous thoughts straight from the devil; at another time he was pressed by lustful desires; at yet another time he even persuaded himself that he was an atheist. There is not a little of John Bunyan's tormenting experience as recorded in *Grace Abounding* in the early spiritual experiences of Charles Spurgeon. But Pilgrim was soon to lose his burden.

In the household of the Newmarket school was a cook, Mary King, a stout old Calvinist of deep religious feelings and strong grasp of the truth. When Spurgeon came under the agony of conviction he sought her counsel. Greatly did she help him—another influence pointing him onward to the Light. "A cook taught me theology!" he used to say in later years. And massive theology too!

His spiritual crisis became intense.

I cried to God with groanings—I say it without exaggeration—groanings that cannot be uttered! and, oh, how I sought in my poor dark way, to overcome first one sin and then another, and so to do better, in God's strength, against the enemies that assailed me, and not, thank God, without success, though still the battle had been lost unless He had come who is the Overcomer of Sin, and the Deliverer of His people, and had put the hosts to flight.

He had, he tells us, become faint, overcome with dread, full of penitence of heart, by reason of two related thoughts—"God's majesty, and my sinfulness." Back home at Colchester for the Christmas holidays, he went questing to various churches seeking Gospel light. He found none, and none of the preachers helped him. One reason for his failure, undoubtedly, was the fact that he held on to his own self-sufficiency, instead of resting entirely on Christ. Another reason was the character of the preaching that he heard. He said:

Though I dearly venerate the men that occupy those pulpits now, and did so then, I am bound to say that I never heard them once preach the Gospel. I mean by that they preached truths, great truths that were fitting to many of their congregation, spiritually minded people; but what I wanted to know was—How can I get my sins forgiven? *And they never once told me that.*

No wonder, in years to come, he was to urge his students that in every sermon there should be something of the Gospel. Deliverance and salvation came to him at length, but only when "God gave me the effectual blow, and I was obliged to submit to that irresistible effort of His grace." God took the initiative in his conversion, as He always does in every true conversion.

Spurgeon's surrender to irresistible grace happened thus. On Sunday, January 6, 1850, a snowy day, he rose before sunrise to pray and read his Bible. But he found no rest for his soul. Later in the morning, with the snow coming down more heavily, he set out for a certain Colchester church recommended by his mother. The fury of the storm, however, compelled him to turn down a side street and, coming upon the Primitive Methodist[10] Church in Artillery Street, he decided to go no further, and turned into the little chapel. It was not the place of his choice, as Dr. W. Y. Fullerton remarks, but it was the place of God's choice. It was the day of deliverance after five weary years in the shadows. There were only fifteen people in the congregation who had braved the snowstorm. Even the appointed minister was snowed up, and the preacher, a thin man with no pretense to education, who could hardly read the Bible aright, entered the pulpit and spoke a few words on the text "Look unto Me, and be ye saved, all the ends of the earth" (Isaiah 45:22). As Spurgeon himself, who had a remarkable memory, recalled it in a sermon in March 1861 at the Metropolitan Tabernacle:

> Blessed be God for that poor local preacher. He read his text. It was as much as he could do. The text was: "Look unto Me, and be ye saved, all the ends of the earth." He was an ignorant man, he could not say much; he was obliged to keep to his text. Thank God for that. He began: "Look, that is not hard work. You need not lift your hand, you do not want to lift your finger. *Look,* a fool can do it. It does not need a wise man to look. A child can do that. It don't need to be full-grown to use your eyes. *Look,* a poor man may do that, no need of riches to look. *Look,* how simple." Then he went on: "Look unto *Me.* Do not look to yourselves, but look to Me, that is Christ. Do not look to God the Father to know whether you are elected or not, you shall find that out afterwards; look to Me, look to Christ. Do not look to God the Holy Spirit to know whether He has called you or not; that you shall discover by and by. Look unto Jesus Christ." And then he went on to put it in his simple way thus: Look unto *Me*; I am sweating great drops of blood for you; look unto *Me,* I am scourged and spit upon; I am nailed to the cross, I die, I am buried, I rise and ascend, I am pleading before the Father's throne, and all this for you.
>
> Now that simple way of putting the Gospel had enlisted my attention, and a ray of light had poured into my heart. Stooping down, he looked under the gallery and said: "Young man, you are very miserable." So I was, but I had not been accustomed to be addressed in that way. "Ah," said he, "and you will always be miserable if you don't do as my text tells you; and that is, Look unto Christ." And then he called out, with all his might, "Young man, look; in God's name look, and look now. Look! Look! Look! You have nothing to do but look and live." I did

---

10. This denomination grew out of the "camp-meeting" movement which was introduced into England by the spectacular wilderness evangelist Lorenzo Dow from America. The Primitive Methodists claimed to return to the *perfectionism* and *evangelism* of John Wesley, both of which they have preserved in their creed but abandoned in practice.

look, blessed be God! I know I looked then and there; and he who but that minute ago had been near despair, had the fullness of joy and hope.

In a moment Charles saw the way of salvation and entered into eternal life. He believed, and was at once engraced into Christ.

The cloud was gone, the darkness rolled away, and in that moment I saw the sun. I had been waiting to do fifty things, but when I heard the word Look, I could almost have looked my eyes away. I could have risen that instant, and sung with the most enthusiastic of them of the precious blood of Christ, and the simple faith that looks alone to Him.

I thought I could dance all the way home. I could understand what John Bunyan meant when he declared he wanted to tell all the crows on the plowed land about his conversion.... Between half past ten, when I entered that chapel and half-past twelve, when I returned home, what a change had taken place in me!

That same evening he went with his mother to the Baptist Chapel at Colchester, and heard a helpful, heartwarming sermon on the text, "Accepted in the Beloved" (Ephesians 1:6). It did much for his assurance of pardon and peace. That same night, when the younger children had gone to bed, Charles told his father of his conversion that morning, and late into the night father and son spoke together of the mighty work of grace on the soul, and of the all-sufficiency of Christ to save and keep and bless.

In the new fervor of his conversion, Charles began to read the Bible with redoubled eagerness. Before long he was convinced that believers were commanded to be baptized by immersion. Writing to his father on the subject after his return to Newmarket, and asking permission to be thus baptized, he said, "From the Scripture, is it not apparent that, immediately upon receiving the Lord Jesus, it is a part of duty to openly profess Him? I firmly believe and consider that baptism is the command of Christ, and shall not feel comfortable if I do not receive it." To his mother he wrote, "Conscience has convinced me that it is a duty to be buried with Christ in baptism, although I am sure that it constitutes no part of salvation." The Catechism of the Church of England also convinced him on this point. He had never even heard of Baptists until he was fourteen, and had heard no sermons on believers' baptism.

He now looked around for a Baptist minister to baptize him. The nearest one was the Rev. W. W. Cantlow of Isleham, a former missionary in Jamaica. On May 3, 1850, his mother's birthday, when he was almost sixteen, he rose early for prayer and walked the eight miles to Isleham Ferry where the Baptismal Service had been arranged to take place. Here the beautiful River Lark flows on its way, dividing Suffolk from Cambridgeshire. It was a Friday, but a goodly number of believers and others had assembled to watch on either shore. Two women were also baptized with Spurgeon, Eunice Fuller and Diana Wilkinson, who ever after delighted in the honor of having been baptized with the Prince of Preachers. The wind was cold, and the river colder still, but Charles's joy in his Lord was at white heat as he was immersed by Mr. Cantlow in the Name of the Trinity, on profession of his faith. From that day Spurgeon ever held believers' baptism in high esteem, and constantly preached its meaning and validity.

That evening was spent at a prayer meeting in the Isleham vestry. The newly baptized boy prayed amongst the rest, and it is recorded that "people wondered and wept for joy as they listened." He returned to Newmarket, and on the following Sunday sat down at the Lord's Table. Before long he was a teacher in the Sunday School. He also found time

Isleham Ferry, Cambridgeshire, where Spurgeon was baptized

to become an energetic distributor of tracts (no doubt some of Mr. Knill's fourteen million), calling usually at about seventy houses on a Saturday afternoon. He was ready to bear testimony by word of mouth also. Seeing a Christian whom he knew about to enter a dancing booth at a village fair, he went up to him and exclaimed, "What doest thou here, Elijah?" The appeal was fruitless, but thus early his Puritan emphasis was evident.

Paul was his hero. In his diary for May 9th he wrote, "Make me to be an eminent servant of Thine, and to be blessed with power to serve Thee like unto Thy great servant Paul." The prayer was abundantly answered. This diary was given to his wife soon after their marriage, with the request that it should not be opened until after his death. She did not open it until 1896, four years after his death. Where is it now? It would be worth a king's ransom! Other extracts may be given: on April 22nd, he wrote, "Went this evening to the prayer-meeting; engaged in prayer. Why should I fear to speak of my only Friend? I shall not be timid another time." At other times he wrote, "Life of my soul, forgive me when I am so blind as to look on an earthly object, and forget Thy divine beauties; Desire of my heart, keep me nearer Thy bosom; Pride is yet my darling sin; Lord, give me much of a Berean nobility."

One final extract from this diary sets the young convert before us as one fully yielded to His Savior: "I vow to glory alone in Jesus, and His cross, and to spend my life in the extension of His cause, in whatsoever way He pleases. I desire to be sincere in this solemn profession, having but one object in view, and that to glorify God. Help me to honor Thee, and live the life of Christ on earth!" How he gloriously fulfilled this desire his whole career gloriously shows.

His first public address, apart from Sunday School talks, was at a missionary meeting in September 1849 and was given at his school. It is recalled by one who heard him that "he spoke fluently." He had been accustomed to missionary activities and to hearing missionaries from his earliest days, and missionary work on sound Gospel lines ever gained his warm interest and support. Indeed, at one time in his early London ministry, he seriously considered whether he was not called to preach Christ in China.

Today, the visitor to the little Methodist Chapel in Artillery Street, Colchester, may read on a tablet these words: "Near this spot C. H. Spurgeon looked and lived." There was the beginning of the great Met-

The Interior of the Artillery Street Methodist Chapel

ropolitan Tabernacle ministry. There was the fountain-head of that mighty river of God of which multitudes in all parts of the world drank and were refreshed.

"Let preachers study this story," recommends Sir William Robertson Nicoll, the great Free Church leader, and former Editor of the *British Weekly*, "Let them believe that under the most adverse circumstances, they may do a good work that will tell on the universe for ever. It was a great thing to have converted Charles Haddon Spurgeon; and who knows but he may have in the smallest and humblest congregation in the world some lad as well worth converting as was he?"

Chapter 3
The Student Pastor

God hath in Himself all power to defend you, all wisdom to direct you, all mercy to pardon you, all grace to enrich you, all righteousness to clothe you, all goodness to supply you, and all happiness to crown you.

—THOMAS BROOKS, *APPLES OF GOLD*

The vocation to the ministry of the Gospel seems to have been pressed upon Spurgeon by the Holy Spirit as early as 1850, when he was sixteen years of age. In a letter to his father he wrote in that year, "How I long for the time when it may please God to make me, like you my father, a successful preacher of the Gospel. Oh that I might see one sinner constrained to come to Jesus! I almost envy you your exalted privileges."

In August 1850 he went to Cambridge as a student-teacher at a school established by Mr. E. S. Leeding, who had been the assistant teacher at the Colchester school when Spurgeon was there. He remained at this establishment for three years without salary, although his board was provided—being supported by the sacrificial gifts of his father and grandfather.

His Puritan sympathies were surely fostered greatly by this stay at Cambridge, the intellectual center in the seventeenth century of the Puritan party in the State. He would gaze at Emmanuel College with loving awe as he recalled that it had nurtured generations of Puritans, many of them the foremost divines of the movement. "The Puritan College," as it was generally called, had been a veritable school of saints. It was founded in 1584 by Sir Walter Mildmay, Chancellor of the

Exchequer and Privy Councillor under Queen Elizabeth the First, and soon became one of the largest and most influential seats of learning in the University.

"Sir Walter," remarked Queen Elizabeth at court one day, "I hear you have erected a Puritan foundation at Cambridge?" "Madam," replied Sir Walter gravely, "far be it from me to countenance anything contrary to Your Majesty's established laws, but I have set an acorn which, when it becomes an oak, God alone knows what will be the fruit of it."

Cambridge

The fruit of Emmanuel College was Puritan teaching and Puritan ministers. Scores of the best Evangelical divines were trained there, including Thomas Brooks, Stephen Charnock, Walter Marshall, Thomas Watson, Edward Clarke, Thomas Shepherd, William Bates, Samuel Clarke, William Bridge, Adoniram Bifield, and Nathaniel Vincent. Although he was barely sixteen, Spurgeon was already familiar with many of these writers. In his "Brief Memoir of Thomas Watson" (which prefaced an edition of Watson's *Body of Divinity* that Spurgeon published), he says of Emmanuel College, that "in those days it deserved to be called the School of Saints, the nursing mother of gigantic Evangelical divines." And he goes on to point out that at least eighty-seven Puritan ministers, including many well known and loved as preachers and commentators, were trained there. In fact he says that the single College of Emmanuel bred more of the Puritans and Nonconformists than perhaps any seven of the other Colleges or Halls in either University."

How he would thrill, also, at the sight of Sidney Sussex College, where that stalwart Puritan soldier and statesman, His Highness the Lord Protector, Oliver Cromwell, was an undergraduate, and many Puritans also; and where Oliver's portrait gazes serenely down in quiet steadfastness from the dining hall wall. Spurgeon ever had an admiration for Cromwell and his Ironsides.

On his first coming to Cambridge he joined St. Andrew's Street Baptist Church, where the famous Robert Hall had ministered, and also Robert Robinson, author of the hymn "Come, Thou fount of every blessing." Spurgeon became active in the Sunday School, and also a member of the Lay Preachers' Association, presided over by a Mr. James Vinter. One Saturday, Mr. Vinter assigned Spurgeon and another lad to take charge of an evening service the next day at the village of Teversham, four miles away. As they walked along the country road, Spurgeon wished his friend God's blessing on his sermon. Dumbfounded, the older man said that he had never preached, and could not preach. He had thought that Spurgeon was to be the preacher. Both were perplexed, and his companion suggested that one of Spurgeon's Sunday School talks would come in useful. Spurgeon thought to himself, "Surely I can tell a few poor cottagers of the sweetness and love of Jesus, since I feel them in my own soul."

Upon arriving at Teversham, they found the meeting place to be in a little thatched cottage, and the congregation consisted of a few farm laborers and their wives. His companion conducted the service, and Spurgeon preached on the text "Unto you therefore which believe He is precious" (1 Peter 2:7). No record remains of what he said, but without doubt he earnestly commended the Lord Jesus as Prophet, Priest, and King, and spoke of the love of Christ to him and to all men. He was thankful that he came to the end of the address without breaking down. His first sermon was surely significant. He was a Christ-centered preacher from the very beginning. Indeed, all through his long ministry he had only one theme—Christ and Him crucified. After the service an aged woman called out, "Bless your dear heart, how old are you?" Spurgeon replied, "I am under sixty." "Yes, and under sixteen," said the old lady. "Never mind my age," replied the boy preacher, "think of Jesus and His preciousness." It was a splendid start.

Soon he was taking other preaching appointments, on weekdays as well as Sundays, and his fame spread throughout the countryside. It was a busy life for a lad. He rose early each morning for prayer and Bible study; then to the school, where he was occupied until five o'clock; and then he set off to some village or other to conduct a service, and tell forth the praises of the Lord Jesus Christ, his Savior. He was immature. He said many odd things, he tells us, and made many blunders, but his mind and heart were full of deep devotion to his Redeemer, and the Lord greatly used him to the blessing and salvation of souls.

One of the places at which he preached regularly was the little Baptist Chapel of Waterbeach, six miles from Cambridge. Surprisingly enough, this is the village where Rowland Hill is said to have preached his first sermon. The homely village congregation were much taken with the youthful Spurgeon, and in spite of his age invited him to be their pastor. They surely had spiritual discernment in so doing. The chapel was small, originally a barn, with a steeply-pitched, thatched roof. The congregation was not large, but they contrived to pay him £45[11] per year. After much prayer and consultation with his father, he accepted the pastorate. He commenced his ministry in January 1852 and remained with them until February 1854. A pastor at sixteen! The ministry there was a signal success and blessing from the start. People flocked from the thatched cottages and farms in the district to the village chapel to hear the boy preacher. In a real sense it was a foreshadowing of his later career.

He continued to reside in lodgings at Cambridge, usually walking to and from Waterbeach. He was a great walker in those days. Waterbeach shaped him, under the good hand of God. He learned the art of handling hard cases—"Perfectionists, half-and-halfers, hypocrites, and misers." Immaturity and pride was neatly taken out of him by painfully frank country folk. Good deacon King, a miller, loved the lad, but toned him down in regard to unguarded speech in the pulpit—a service for which many an experienced preacher would be the better. He made friends with Pastor Cornelius Elvin of Bury St. Edmunds who, on a visit to Waterbeach for a minister's Anniversary service, said to him, "Lad, study hard; keep abreast of your foremost Christians; for if they outstrip you in the knowledge of Scripture, or power to edify, they will be dissatisfied with your ministry!" "That spur was useful," Spurgeon commented. But they never did outstrip him in this; no one ever did, then or later.

His first convert was a laborer's wife, and how he prized that soul. Early on the Monday morning he called at her cottage for a pastoral word with his spiritual child. "If anyone had said to me," he afterwards related, "'Somebody has left you twenty thousand pounds,' I should not have given a snap of my fingers for it compared with the joy which I felt when I was told that God had saved a soul through my ministry. I felt like a diver who had been down to the depth of the sea and brought up a rare pearl."

Writing to his mother he speaks with gratitude of the progress of the church, and of how happy he was in the midst of a loving people.

I have all that my heart can wish for; yes, God gives more than my desire. My congregation is as great and loving as ever. During all the

---

11. The monetary unit used in the United Kingdom is the pound sterling, which is indicated by the following symbol: £. Throughout this book the cost of building materials, wages, gifts, etc. are given in the original currency of the times. In order to translate these values into present equivalents of any particular country or time period, the reader may use as a norm the wages paid to a skilled worker which was then about £100 annually.

time I have been at Waterbeach I have had a different house for my home every day. Fifty-two families have thus taken me in; and I have still six other invitations not yet accepted. Talk about the people not caring for me because they give me so little! I dare tell anybody under heaven 'tis false! They do all they can. Our anniversary passed off grandly: six were baptized; crowds on crowds stood by the river; the chapel afterwards was crammed both to the tea and the sermon.

But if Waterbeach shaped him, it can be said that he, through God's gracious power, transformed Waterbeach. His evangelical passion increased. In a few weeks the little chapel was packed to the doors. The membership jumped from forty to a hundred—quite remarkable for a village church. It was the ancient miracle of the Spirit honoring a lad with a blameless life and a mighty message. Reprobates, scoffers, drunkards, were reclaimed and transformed. Christ and Him crucified, proclaimed with simplicity allied to passion by a boy of sixteen, did wondrous things. Preaching on March 30, 1862, at the Metropolitan Tabernacle he said:

I received some years ago orders from my Master to stand at the foot of the cross until He came. He has not come yet, but I mean to stand there till He does. If I should disobey His orders and leave those simple truths which have been the means of the conversion of souls, I know not how I could expect His blessing. It is of Christ I love to speak—of Christ Who loved, and lived, and died, the substitute for sinners, the just for the unjust, that He might bring us to God.... I knew a village once that was perhaps one of the worst villages in England for many things; where many an illicit distillery was yielding its noxious liquor to a manufacturer without payment of the duty to the Government, and where in connection with that all manner of riot and iniquity were rife. There went a lad into that village, and but a lad, and one who had no scholarship, but was rough and sometimes vulgar. He began to preach there, and it pleased God to turn that village upside down, and in a short time the little thatched chapel was crammed, and the biggest vagabonds of the village were weeping floods of tears, and those who had been the curse of the parish became its blessing; and where there had been robberies and villainies of every kind all round the neighborhood, there were none, because the men who did the mischief were themselves in the house of God, rejoicing to hear of Jesus crucified. Mark me, I am not telling you an exaggerated story now, nor a thing that I do not know. Yet this one thing I remember to the praise of God's grace, it pleased the Lord to work signs and wonders in our midst. He showed the power of Jesus' name, and made us witnesses of that Gospel which can win souls, draw reluctant hearts, and mold the life and conduct of men afresh.

Note the modesty of that account, and how all the glory is given to the Lord. The simple hearted folk of Waterbeach gave the lad their hearts without reserve, and he responded with the utmost he knew of the Gospel story and the manifold counsel of God.

The afternoon service at Waterbeach (there was no evening service in those days because of the difficulty of lighting the building) followed quickly after the morning service, with only a short interval for dinner. One Sunday after dinner, Spurgeon could not recall even the subject of the sermon he had prepared for the second service. "Oh, never mind," said his farmer host, "you will be sure to have a good word for us." At that moment a blazing log fell out of the fire. "There," said his host, "is a sermon for you. "Is not this a brand plucked out of the fire?" And on that text Spurgeon preached with converting power.

His brother James came to stay with him, and accompanied him on his preaching appointments. Years later he recollected:

> When I drove my brother about the country to preach, I thought then, as I have thought ever since, what an extraordinary preacher he was. What wonderful zeal and power I remember in some of those early speeches! The effect upon the people listening to him I have never known exceeded in after years. He seemed to have leaped full-grown into the pulpit. The breadth and brilliance of those early sermons, and the power that God's Holy Spirit evidently gave to him, made them perfectly marvelous. When he went to Waterbeach his letters came home, and were read as family documents, discussed, prayed over, and wondered at. We were not surprised, however, for we all believed it was in him.

It was his intense devotion to his Savior; it was his wonderful knowledge of the Word of God; it was his grasp of great and vital doctrines; and it was his deep passion for the salvation of souls, that combined to make him a mighty instrument in the hands of the Lord. And if we, in these flabby and degenerate days, are to be effective and fruitful in the proclamation of the Gospel, we shall have to get back to these fundamental and all essential things.

Thoughts of a theological college training arose in his mind from time to time. Both his father and grandfather were in favor of it. He was not altogether convinced of the usefulness of this course, but was somewhat inclined towards it. At length an appointment was made for him to be interviewed by Dr. Joseph Angus, Principal of Stepney College, London (now Regent's Park Baptist College, Oxford), who was to preach at Cambridge. The interview with Dr. Angus was to be at the home of Mr. Macmillan the publisher, whose firm was then established in the University town. At the appointed hour Spurgeon was at the house, and the maid showed him into the drawing-room.

He waited there for two hours, but felt too much of his own insignificance to ring the bell and inquire about the cause of the delay. When at

The young preacher

last he did ring, it was to be informed that Dr. Angus, who had been shown into another room, had waited awhile and then been compelled to leave in order to catch a train for London. The servant girl had not told anyone in the house of the young man's arrival, and so the two men had missed each other. (But they were to meet years later in singular circumstances, as we shall relate.)

At first, Spurgeon was much disappointed at this unusual happening, but he came to regard it as having been Providential—had he not read the Puritan classic, Flavel's *Mystery of Providence?*—and as an illustration of the text, "The steps of a good man are ordered of the Lord." Characteristically, Spurgeon amended this to "the *stops* of a good man are ordered of the Lord!" On the afternoon of this frustrating day, he was on his way to a preaching appointment at Chesterton, and in crossing Midsummer Common a voice said clearly to him, "Seekest thou great things for thyself? Seek them not." Then and there he renounced all thought of a collegiate course. Years later we find him saying:

> From that first day until now, I have acted on no other principle but that of perfect consecration to the work whereunto I am called. I surrendered myself to my Savior, I gave Him my body, my soul, my spirit—for eternity! I gave him my talents, my powers, my eyes, my ears, my whole manhood. So far from regretting what I then did, I would gladly renew my vows and make them over again!

And thus, at the morning of eighteen, he was wholly yielded to His Lord, and ready for anything the Master might have for him to do. It is vain to speculate as to the difference a theological college course would have made to Spurgeon. No doubt it would not have damaged his evangelical fervor, but it might have deadened, while it educated, his style. In any case, all his life Spurgeon was a great reader and student, and to say, as some have said, that he had an undisciplined and untrained mind is sheer nonsense. He more than made up by his prodigious reading all he may have missed at college.

The Rev. James Douglas, MA, one of his later friends, has this to say:

> There was nothing in him necessitating delay! He could be placed in the seat of Honor, for he had the spiritual grounding requisite. The light was there, it needed but a stand adequate to its power of illumination. He had foresworn the search of great things for himself, and what is this in the economy of grace, but the forerunner of promotion?

The busy streets of London

Chapter 4
London Calls

In settling you in such an employment and calling in the world, as possibly neither yourselves nor parents could ever expect you should attain to.... How strangely are things wheeled about by Providence. Not what we or our parents, but what God designed shall take place. Amos was very humbly employed at first, but God designed him for a more honorable and comfortable calling.

—JOHN FLAVEL, *THE MYSTERY OF PROVIDENCE*

London was bound to hear of the powerful young Cambridgeshire preacher sooner or later. Perhaps, if matters had taken a normal course, he would have proceeded to a bigger church in a country town, and then gone to a London congregation. But God ordered otherwise, and used a very curious incident to set events in action, or "wheel it about" as Flavel would say.

In the summer of 1853 he was one of the speakers at the Annual Meeting of the Cambridge Sunday School Union in the ancient Guildhall. Here a most extraordinary scene occurred. Spurgeon's extreme youth (he was only nineteen) caused two of the subsequent ministerial speakers publicly and rudely to make very insulting and contemptuous references to him. One of them asked why he had left his few sheep in the wilderness; while the other said loftily that boys should tarry at Jericho until their beards were grown before they attempted to instruct their seniors. Dr. Fullerton says that they spoke thus "in the manners of the time." This is simply incredible. They were Christians, speaking at a meeting of Christians, having a different spirit from the world. They acted disgracefully. No doubt their appalling conduct was due to jealousy. Spurgeon quite rightly asked permission to reply, and reminded his hearers that the individuals referred to in Scripture were men, whose beards had been shaved off by their enemies, not boys; and that an old man who had disgraced his calling resembled them more than a young minister who was seeking faithfully to fulfill it. This shot hit the mark, for one of the speakers had fallen into sin and cast a shadow over his ministry. The audience very readily took the point, and agreed with Spurgeon.

It so happened—"in the Providence of God"—that a Mr. George Gould from Loughton, Essex, was at the meeting, and was deeply impressed both by Spurgeon's address, and also the grand way in which he had answered and discomforted his detractors. On his return home, he urged Thomas Olney, a friend of his and a deacon at New Park Street Baptist Chapel, London, to secure Spurgeon's services for their vacant pulpit. Thomas Olney wrote in due course, addressing the letter to the Chapel at Waterbeach.

On arriving at the chapel on the last Sunday of November 1853, Spurgeon found Mr. Olney's letter waiting for him. He was amazed as he read the invitation to preach in the important London church. Passing the letter to Robert Coe, one of the deacons, he declared that it must be a mistake, the letter could not be meant for him. The deacon sorrowfully shook his head; it was no mistake, he was sure. What he had long dreaded had come to pass, another bigger church was trying to steal their pastor away from them.

Next day, Spurgeon sent a timid reply, expressing willingness to come to preach in London, but suggesting that a mistake may have been made, as he was only nineteen and quite unknown. The reply from Mr. Olney confirmed the earlier letter; there had been no mistake. So Spurgeon arranged to preach at New Park Street, Southwark, on December 18, 1853.

New Park Street Baptist Chapel was one of the three leading churches of the 113 belonging to the Baptist denomination in the London area. At that time it had a membership on the roll of 313, but its Sunday congregations had been reduced until they were quite small. It was the largest of the Baptist Church buildings, seating 1,200 persons, but it was a dwindling cause.

It was an historic church. During its two hundred years history it had had three outstanding preachers. Benjamin Keach, who had suffered in the pillory[12] for his faith, was Pastor for thirty-six years from 1668-1704. Dr. John Gill was minister for fifty-one years, from 1720-1771, and was the author of a voluminous and learned commentary, long outdated. Dr. John Rippon, famous for his hymnbook, ministered for no less than sixty-three years, from 1773-1836. Dr. Rippon had come to be Pastor when only twenty years of age, a fact that brought no little comfort to Spurgeon. Since his days several other ministers had labored there, but without much success, and the congregation was only about 200. The pastorate had been vacant for three months, but none of the candidates for the pulpit so far had been asked to preach a second time!

Benjamin Keach in the Pillory

The geographical position of the church was unfavorable. It stood in the low-lying Southwark district, in a dingy, repellent section of the town, often river-flooded. It was, in fact, very much a downtown chapel, in a gloomy, narrow street, surrounded by poor, dirty houses,

---

12. A device consisting of a wooden board with holes for the head and hands, in which petty offenders were formerly locked and exposed to public scorn.

grimy factories, and sprawling warehouses. The direct road to it lay over Southwark Bridge, where a toll was charged. No wonder the people moved away to more wholesome regions, and that the church was in decline.

On Saturday, December 17th, Spurgeon arrived in London by the Eastern Counties Railway. He had a distinctly countrified appearance, rural clothes, large black satin tie, and a blue handkerchief with white spots. (This handkerchief got him into trouble, for he flourished it vigorously during preaching—a habit they had not been accustomed to. The deacons tactfully gave him a dozen white handkerchiefs, later.) The young preacher was installed in a Bloomsbury boarding-house, as apparently none of the members were able to give him hospitality in their own homes. The other boarders looked in amazement at his round cheeks and country clothes, and talked impressively of the famous preachers of London—Dr. Brook, Dr. Stearne, Dr. Stovel, and many more. Wonderful men, and every one a Doctor of Divinity! Spurgeon went to bed somewhat depressed, and could not sleep because of the noise of the traffic.

Sunday morning, December 18th, dawned clear and cold. He walked to New Park Street through a wilderness of buildings, with scarcely a tree to be seen, and on arrival was much impressed by the chapel's imposing appearance. Surely there would be a wealthy and critical congregation. The morning congregation was sparse indeed, about eighty people, far fewer than gathered at his thatched chapel at Waterbeach. (How were they getting on, he wondered?) The Lord gave him confidence. He preached from the text, "Every good gift, and every perfect gift, is from above, and cometh down from the Father of lights, with whom is no variableness, neither shadow of turning" (James 1:17). Unusual interest was taken in the sermon, in spite of the disliked handkerchief waving. One of the deacons said that if the preacher were only with them for three months the place would be crowded. A prophecy indeed!

During the afternoon, numbers of the congregation called on their friends and urged them to be present at the evening service. They had a preacher of remarkable power in spite of his youth. They had never heard the like of it. A greatly increased number gathered at night, amongst them the young girl destined to be his future wife. He preached from the text, "They are without fault before the Throne of

God" (Revelation 14:5). The effect was tremendous. The spotted hand-kerchief, though vigorously used, was hardly noticed. What eloquence! What knowledge of the Bible! What love for Christ! What zeal for souls! They were absolutely captivated by him. They were loath to let him go. The people were too excited to leave the building and stood about in groups discussing the sermon, the preacher, and the vacant pastorate. This was the man for them! Not a doubt of it. The deacons were but-tonholed and urged to secure the young man at once. Not for a long time had the congregation heard Christ so preached, His love pressed home to the heart and conscience, the Gospel plan of redemption made so plain. It was to them as one of the days of the Most High. They must have him for their minister at all costs!

Spurgeon's own account of the day is as follows:

> The Lord helped me very graciously, I had a happy Sabbath in the pul-pit, and spent the interval with warm-hearted friends; and when at night I trudged back to the Queen's Square narrow lodging, I was not alone, and I no longer looked on Londoners as hard-hearted barbari-ans. My tone was altered, I wanted no pity of anyone; I did not care a penny for the young gentleman lodgers and their assessment of the renown preachers of London, nor for the grind of the cabs, nor for anything else under the sun. The lion had been looked at all round, and his majesty did not appear to be a tenth as majestic as when I had only heard his roar miles away.

The next day he spent seeing the sights of London, during which he climbed to the top of St. Paul's Cathedral, and bought a set of Thomas Scott's famous Commentary. Rather surprisingly, he came to have a poor opinion of Scott, though the work is a faithful exposition and full of spiritual meat. London, at that time, was barely a quarter of its present size. The outer suburbs were still rural retreats. Stagecoaches drove into town from the suburbs and neighboring places, though their days were numbered. Horse-drawn carriages and wagons filled the streets. Great areas of slums abounded, and it was estimated that no less than 3,000 children under fourteen were living as thieves and beg-gars, and over 100,000 were without education of any kind. But reform was on the way. Lord Shaftesbury was leading a crusade against many evils and a better social day was in sight. So too were orphanages, though the young preacher from Cambridgeshire had not a thought about them as yet.

Spurgeon's relationship with the New Park Street Chapel was quickly consolidated. He paid three more visits on Sundays in January 1854, and was then invited to occupy the pulpit for six months on probation, with a view to the permanent acceptance of the pastorate. Spurgeon pondered this situation and consulted his father. It was strongly impressed upon him that he should not accept an unqualified invitation to supply the pulpit for so long a time.

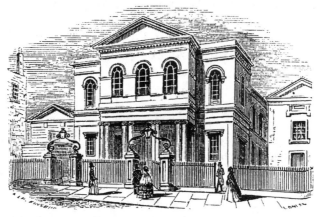

New Park Street Chapel

"My objection," he wrote, "is not to the length of the time of probation, but it ill becomes a youth to promise to preach to a London congregation so long until he knows them and they know him. I would engage to supply for three months of that time, and then, should the congregation fail or the church disagree, I would reserve to myself the liberty, without breach of engagement, to retire, and you on your part would have the right to dismiss me without seeming to treat me ill. Enthusiasm and popularity are often like the crackling of thorns, and soon expire. I do not wish to be a hindrance if I cannot be a help."

The congregation agreed to this, and Spurgeon began his famous ministry on the first Sunday in March 1854. So, humanly speaking, the insufferable rudeness of two so-called Christian ministers, was the cause of his becoming a greatly used London preacher. "God moves in a mysterious way His wonders to perform." He certainly "wheeled about" events in order to bring to pass His foreordained purpose.

There is no record, alas, of his first sermons on commencing his wonderful ministry in London. But without doubt he preached Christ in all the wonders of His grace, and in all the fullness of His truth, as Savior of sinners and Redeemer of lives. The wooing note of the Gospel and the stern note of Judgment to come were perfectly balanced in his powerful and Spirit-filled ministry.

He took lodgings at 75 Dover Road, Southwark. Deep sorrow at parting from him was shown by his county flock at Waterbeach, but beyond this there is no record of the farewell. Or did Spurgeon not have a farewell, thinking that perhaps he would be back with them before long? As a matter of fact he was to return and preach to them on several occasions in the future, wonderful times, too, when the little thatched chapel could not contain the people who wished to hear him, and when he had to speak to them in a field.

Earnestly did he seek the Lord's help for his new sphere, and pressed on with all his youthful evangelical zeal to win souls in dark and needy London. From the very beginning he felt it to be a mission field. "Our place," he wrote to his grandparents at Stambourne—(ah, how they prayed for him, and Aunt Ann too!) "is one of the pinnacles of the denomination. But I have a great work to do, and have need of all the prayers the sons of God can offer for me." He had them in plenty from the New Park Street people, some of whom banded themselves together to pray every day for their young minister.

A few weeks after his first Sunday as pastor, a new development took place. Fifty men of the church prepared a signed petition to the deacons demanding a special church meeting. At this session, amid tremendous enthusiasm, the members passed a resolution placing on record the great esteem in which the preacher was held, the extraordinary increase in the congregation both on Lord's Days and weekdays and "consider it prudent to secure as early as possible his permanent settlement amongst us." On April 28th Spurgeon replied, "There is but one answer to so loving and candid an invitation. I accept it." He went on to ask for their prayers, and added, "Remember my youth and inexperience and pray that these may not hinder my usefulness. I trust also the remembrance of these will lead you to forgive mistakes I may make, or unguarded words that I may utter." A spirit of becoming humility was not the least of the graces that the Lord had given him.

And so this historic pastoral settlement was made, manifestly under the hand and in the will of God. Never did the people regret it, and only once or twice, on account of extraordinary trials, did he have any misgivings. The union of Pastor and people thus begun lasted until his death in 1892, no less than thirty-eight years. It was a success in the highest sense right from the start, as all true ministries should be. Never has London, or anywhere else, seen such a God-honoring, Christ-exalting, Spirit-filled, Bible-based, soul-winning ministry. A ministry consecrated to the dual task of bringing together the sinner and his Savior, the saint and His Lord. It shook hard, selfish, pagan London to its foundations; it quickened ministries and churches in Evangelical life in all denominations and in all parts of the land; it established a criterion of ministry loved, honored, and striven for by thousands ever since. Truly, there was a man sent from God whose name was Charles Haddon Spurgeon.

One of the earliest to discern the pulpit greatness of Spurgeon was James Sheridan Knowles, the Irish dramatist and actor. He had trained for the medical profession and obtained the degree of MD, but later forsook medicine for the stage. He was a popular actor, especially in Ireland, and wrote a number of plays. Among his friends he numbered Lamb, Coleridge, and Hazlitt. For a time he was the Lessee of Drury Lane Theatre. In later years he was converted and became a Baptist preacher, drawing large crowds to Exeter Hall and elsewhere. He was teacher of elocution at Stepney Baptist College. One day he entered his classroom and said excitedly:

"Boys, have you heard the Cambridgeshire preacher?" None of them had. "Go and hear him at once," cried Knowles, "his name is Charles Spurgeon. He is only a boy, but he is the most wonderful preacher in the world. He is absolutely perfect in oratory, and beside that a master in the art of acting. He has nothing to learn from me or anyone else. He is simply perfect. He knows everything. He can do anything. I was once lessee of Drury Lane Theatre; were I still in that position I would offer him a fortune to play for a season on the boards of that house. Why boys, he can do anything he pleases with his audience! He can make them laugh and cry and laugh again in five minutes. His power was never equaled."

And Knowles went on to declare that Spurgeon would live to be the greatest preacher of the age, and that his name would be known everywhere. This was an appraisal of one whose judgment was worth a great deal; it was also a remarkable prophecy.

Great preacher though he was, he was also a true pastor, two functions not always to be found in the same individual. In 1854, only a few months after his arrival in London, an epidemic of Asiatic cholera visited his part of the city, and many of his congregation were smitten down. He visited family after family, bringing prayer and comfort. Many times each week he stood by someone's grave. It was a dark and harrowing experience for one so young and new to his work. He was sent for by persons of all ranks and religions. He became weary in body and sick at heart. He felt that the burden was more than he could bear. But God was at hand to revive his spirit. Returning sadly from a funeral one day, he noticed a sheet of paper stuck up in a shoemaker's shop. In bold hand writing were the words, "Because thou hast made the Lord, which is my refuge, thy habitation, there shall no evil befall thee, neither shall any plague come nigh thy dwelling." The effect on his heart was immediate. He received the message as the Word of God for his own soul in his burdensome situation. He felt secure, refreshed, endowed with immortality. Lines from an old hymn recurred to him:

> *Not a single shaft can hit,*
> *Till the God of love sees fit.*

He remembered Cromwell's oft-repeated phrase, "Man is immortal till his work is done." He went on with his visitation of the sick and dying in a calm and peaceful spirit. He felt no fear of evil; he suffered no harm.

But now a new, sweet influence entered his life. Amongst the hearers of the young preacher at his first service at New Park Street was Miss Susannah Thompson, daughter of Mr. Robert Thompson, of Falcon Square. She was not particularly impressed by him at first. It is not recorded what she thought of that terrible spotted handkerchief which he waved about. She was, in fact, at their first meeting, what Cromwell described his own daughter to be "a seeker." She very soon became a happy "finder" under his Christ-filled ministry. She was of slight stature, her oval face framed in long chestnut curls, and she was twenty-two. Her hazel eyes held a captivating light, and they captivated Charles. Very much so! They met several times at the home of Thomas Olney, his senior deacon. The friendship ripened swiftly. Before long he was deeply in love, and she with him. He sent her a copy of Bunyan's *Pilgrim's Progress* inscribed, "Miss Thompson, with desires for her

progress in the blessed pilgrimage, C. H. Spurgeon, April 20, 1854." He
was eager for her to drink of the Puritan well from which so often he
had satisfied his thirst. A little later she gave him, as one of her first gifts,
a complete set of the works of John Calvin! (Father probably paid, as
they would be expensive.) She wrote him a letter asking for church
membership and stating her Christian experience, as was the happy
custom of the time. He replied in truly old-world style: "Dear purchase
of a Savior's blood, you are to me a Savior's gift, and my heart is full to
overflowing with the thought of such continual goodness." From which
we may learn that it was not only the addition of another member to
his church that rejoiced his heart, but the prospect of an intimate union
of heart with the young lady of his choice. He baptized her at New Park
Street on February 1, 1855.

On June 10, 1854, they were together at the brilliant opening of the
Crystal Palace, moved piece by piece from Hyde Park to the heights of
Norwood, near where he was later to live. They sat together in the
grandstand never thinking that on that very spot, in days to come, he
would preach to the largest congregation ever assembled since the days
of George Whitefield, his hero and model. Charles carried a book, but
not one of deep divinity, but of poetry. He was always fond of poetry.
He got Susannah to read one of the poems, chosen by himself, on the
subject of love and marriage, and slyly whispered to her: "Do you pray
for him who is to be your husband?" Susannah's heart beat fast, she
blushed and lowered her gaze, but did not answer. They drifted away
from their party and wandered through the extensive grounds together.
In August, in her grandmother's garden (he was a romantic), he proposed and was accepted. During the next twelve months they were constantly together when his duties would allow, and collaborated in
compiling a small book of choice spiritual extracts from one of his
favorite Puritan authors, Thomas Brooks. It was published under the
playful title of *Smooth Stones from Old Brooks*, hardly respectful
enough, some might think. It has hardly been heard of since, but is a
rare and valuable collector's item. Brooks is best read in the original!
Later that year he sent her a copy of his first volume of sermons, with
the inscription: "In a few days it will be out of my power to present anything to *Miss Thompson*. Let this be a remembrance of our happy meetings and sweet conversations. C. H. Spurgeon." He could not have
conceived the extraordinary extent to which his printed sermons

would be circulated, and the effect they would have all over the world in the blessing and salvation of souls.

They were married on January 8, 1856, at New Park Street Chapel, by Dr. Alexander Fletcher of Finsbury Chapel. Two thousand people crowded into the chapel, and hundreds thronged the street. His mother and father were there, and brother James and Aunt Ann from Stambourne. Also, of course, a host of relatives of the bride with the chestnut curls. The hymn sung was most appropriate for his evangelical labors, "Salvation, O the joyful sound," by Isaac Watts. The honeymoon was spent in Paris—not, one would have thought, the sort of place in which a Puritan would honeymoon! But they enjoyed it, and it was not to be his last visit, either.

God had certainly made them for each other. It was a love match, but also a spiritual partnership, as every true Christian marriage should be. Heavily did they lean upon one another. Closely were their hearts and aims entwined. Richly did the Lord bless and use them together. And although, sad to relate, for most of her married life Susannah was an invalid, and had to serve behind the scenes; and though his incessant labors kept them much apart, yet their love grew in beauty and in tenderness through the years. She called him *Tir-shatha*—Hebrew for "The Reverence," a title given to Zerubbabel and Nehemiah as governors of Judah under the King of Persia. He called her "Angel and Delight," and was never happier than when devising some scheme or gift to give her pleasure.

The young couple took up residence first at 217 New Kent Road, and then, after the birth of twin sons, Charles and Thomas, on September 20, 1856, they removed to a large house, "Helensburgh," in Nightingale Lane, Clapham. Here there was an extensive garden, which greatly delighted them, and the wide spaces of Clapham Common, green and leafy, and reminding him of the country a little. In 1886 the old "Helensburgh" was completely demolished and a lovely two-story house of gray brick erected in its place. The chief part of the cost was defrayed by a few of Spurgeon's friends. While the house was being built, the Spurgeons lived at Brighton.

During the early years of Spurgeon's ministry at New Park Street and the Metropolitan Tabernacle, Susannah was very active as helpmeet to her Charles. Visiting the congregation, shepherding the female candidates at baptisms, writing letters for him before he had a secretary, entertaining large numbers of visitors at home, including some famous ones like John Ruskin, a great admirer of Spurgeon, and some of those wonderful Doctors of Divinity about whom he had heard so much on his first day in London. (But they did not seem so remarkable at first hand, he thought!) Moreover, she laid the foundation stone of the Pastors' College, which he inaugurated for the training of Gospel ministers. And she started her Book Fund, beginning with five-shilling pieces which she saved, which was to supply copies of her husband's books and of sound Evangelical and Puritan works (including *Old Brooks)* to needy ministers. There were a good many of these, alas, and it took a great deal of money to supply them, but she raised it somehow, thousands of pounds all told during her lifetime, and many a struggling country pastor had cause to bless God for her kind gifts.

She delighted to read the Puritans to him on Saturday nights. Those were the days when reading aloud was one of the quiet delights of the long evenings in the pre-radio and TV era, and they got through a tremendous amount of solid, heart-warming seventeenth-century literature together. Much of it went all unconsciously into his sermons. She sacrificed many comforts so that her "Tirshatha" might start his college, but she did not hesitate. It was not just for him, it was for the Lord. Many times he came home from his services exhausted and dispirited. But she knew a sovereign remedy; she would read to him from Baxter's *Reformed Pastor,* and he would be strong again. What she meant to him may be gleaned from a letter he wrote her in 1889, during the "Down Grade"[13]" controversy. "You are as an angel of God to me.... Bravest of women, strong in the faith, you have ministered unto me.... God bless thee out of the Seventh Heaven!" if it is true that behind every good man there is a good woman, then it is surely true of C. H. Spurgeon. God surely gave her to him for his strength and comfort, and sweetly and mightily did she fulfill her great task and privilege. Susannah Spurgeon, across the years, we salute you!

---

13. This controversy arose over the departure of many ministers from Calvinistic doctrine and vital Evangelical emphases; this was due to the impact of the so-called Higher Criticism of the Scriptures and of the rationalistic theology coming out of Germany, and of Darwin's theory of biological evolution. (*See chapter 11.*)

Chapter 5
"Over the Water to Charlie"

The work of conversion is the first and great thing we must drive at; after this we must labour with all our might. Alas, the misery of the unconverted is so great, that it calleth loudest to us for compassion. They are in the gall of bitterness, and in the bond of iniquity, and have no part nor fellowship in the pardon of their sins, or the hope of glory.... Methinks if by faith we did indeed look upon them as within a step of hell, it would more effectually untie our tongues, than Croesus' danger,[14] as they tell us, did his son's.

—RICHARD BAXTER, *THE REFORMED PASTOR*

Crowds! Thousands upon thousands! Streaming along the pavements, filling the roads, coming in carriages. Eager, excited, milling crowds. Rich and poor, young and old, professionals and peasants. What had brought them to New Park Street Chapel, or wherever else Spurgeon preached? It was his youth. It was his earnestness. It was his unaffected simplicity. It was his oratorical power. It was his intense devotion to his Redeemer. It was the power of the Holy Spirit. Drawn as to a magnet they flocked to him. Throngs, multitudes, double-squeezed into the varnished pews, peering in at the doors, crowding the aisles, squatting

14. Croesus, the last king of the ancient Lydia (6th century B.C.), was about to be killed by a Persian soldier, when the horror of the sight loosened the tongue of Croesus' dumb son, and he cried, "Fellow, slay not Croesus."

on the pulpit stairs, perched like starlings on the windowsills.

The conductors of the horse-drawn buses on the north side of the Thames, on Sunday mornings, used to entice people into their vehicles with the shout, "Over the water to Charlie!," and with what eagerness they clambered aboard.

London Bridge

Crowds, and yet more crowds! It was a wonder that it did not turn his head. But not for nothing was Spurgeon the "heir of the Puritans." He knew himself to be the God-appointed messenger of eternal truth. His work was done "in the great Taskmaster's eye," as Milton had long ago taught him. He had a heaven to win or lose as other men, and the honor of Christ lay upon him, as Richard Baxter in *The Reformed Pastor* constantly reminded him. Indeed, he had taken deeply to heart Baxter's warnings against pride, and his emphasis on humility. And although he was soon the talk of the town, indeed of the whole country, he was so steeped in the Puritan view of things that he was kept unspoiled, and "meet for the Master's use."

Four years after coming to London the foundation stone of the great Metropolitan Tabernacle was laid, in August 1859. (A later chapter will deal with this great event.) Beneath the stone was placed an account of the history of the church to that date, and concerning the new ministry of Charles Haddon Spurgeon. Regarding the latter, a very significant word is used: Revival!

From the day he commenced his labors in our midst, it pleased the Lord our God to grant us a Revival *which has steadily progressed ever since....* So did the Holy Ghost accompany the preaching of the Gospel with divine power, that almost every sermon proved the means of awakening and regeneration to some who were hitherto "dead in trespasses and sins."

Revival—continuous revival! Almost every sermon leading to conversions. The Lord was with him, and let none of his words fall to the ground! This was in fact the condition and atmosphere of the church right to the end of Spurgeon's ministry. The atmosphere of the services was charged with soul-saving, Christ-exalting power. The Holy Spirit brooded over the meetings, and thousands upon thousands were led to a saving knowledge of Christ and added to the flock of the Redeemer. The foundation stone statement went on to assert:

Every attempt to trace the popular demand for evangelical teaching to spasmodic excitement has failed. The pastor of New Park Street Church has never consciously departed from the simple rule of faith recorded in the New Testament. The doctrines he has set forth are identical with those which have been received by godly men of every section of the Church since the days of the Apostles. The services of religion have been conducted without any peculiarity or innovation. No musical or aesthetic accompaniments have ever been used. "The weapons of our warfare are not carnal, but they are mighty."

Neither, be it noted, were the crowds drawn in by the mass advertising associated with much present-day evangelism. There were no large pictures of Spurgeon on the billboards. The crowds came hungry for spiritual food, and he fed them with the Bread of Life. No posters, no leaflets, no loudspeakers. The people told one another that the Lord was with him, and they came.

Sometimes, it is true, there were comparatively dry periods, but they did not last long. One month, for instance, only seven new members joined the church. One of the deacons said to him: "This won't pay, Guv'nor, running all this big place for seven new members in a month. This won't do...!" And we are sometimes elated if we get seven new members in as many years. One Sunday in December 1858 the Surrey Gardens crowd dwindled to very small proportions, and Spurgeon appeared sad. But the next Sunday the crowds came back.

Crowds, but he remembered both faces and names in a most

extraordinary way. When in February 1888 at the Metropolitan Tabernacle he preached on the text: "He calleth His own sheep by name, and leadeth them out" (John 10:3), he said: "I used to have such a trustworthy memory that I not only knew the nearly 6,000 members of this church by face, which I am still able to do, but I knew them all by name, and it was a rare thing for me ever to forget or make a mistake!"

New Park Street Chapel, which he had once thought was "hopelessly large," seating twelve hundred, soon proved to be hopelessly small. One night when the building was painfully jammed, Spurgeon turned to the wall behind the pulpit and declared: "By faith the walls of Jericho fell down, and by faith this wall shall come down, too." The deacons were not too pleased with the proposal, but Spurgeon had his way as he nearly always did. The wall came down. Two thousand pounds were spent in enlarging the Chapel, and building a new school room at the side whose sliding windows could be opened so that people there could hear. The alterations lasted from February 11th until May 27, 1855, and during the work the services were held in Exeter Hall in the Strand.

This was a famous auditorium holding 4,500 people, where the May meetings of various Christian societies were held. It stood at the very heart of the metropolis, and from the beginning the hall was crowded. For six Sundays the streets were choked with people, vehicles having to come to a halt, pedestrians buffeted and pushed, and the police almost helpless to deal with the situation. This first great experience of preaching to enormous crowds was a great trial to Spurgeon, and a drain upon his energies, but gradually, by the grace of God, he became accustomed to them, and to be their master. He also learned how to control that beautiful voice of his.

With increasing popularity came opposition. Resenting the attacks made on his kingdom, the devil raged against the boy preacher. Certain sections of the press were particularly violent. Certain jealous ministers in the suburbs, who were losing part of their congregations to him, fanned the flame of hatred, ridicule, and contempt. But, like Nehemiah of old, Spurgeon took refuge in prayer and trust in the mighty hand of God. Two of his most bitter detractors, who certainly should have known better, were *The Saturday Review* and *Punch*. Derogatory paragraphs and satirical cartoons appeared regularly in these and other journals. Dr. Alexander Whyte once told how, in the days of his early poverty, he, with a number of other lads subscribed to buy *Punch*, but

Spurgeon preaching at Exeter Hall, 1855

they dropped it because of what seemed to them its unjust caricatures of the great preacher. The following quotation from a Sheffield paper is typical of the view that was generally expressed:

> Just now, the great lion, star, meteor, or whatever else he may be called, of the Baptists, is the Rev. Mr. Spurgeon, minister of Park Street Chapel, Southwark. He has created a perfect *furor* in the religious world. Every Sunday, crowds throng to Exeter Hall, as to some great dramatic entertainment. The huge hall is crowded to overflowing with an excited auditory, whose good fortune in obtaining admission is often envied by the hundreds outside who throng the closed doors.... Mr. Spurgeon preaches himself. He is nothing unless he is an actor, unless exhibiting that matchless impudence which is his great charac-

teristic, indulging in coarse familiarity with holy things, declaiming in a ranting and colloquial style, strutting up and down the platform as though he were at the Surrey Theater, and boasting of his own intimacy with Heaven with nauseating frequency.... It would seem that the poor young man's brain is turned by the notoriety he has acquired and the incense offered at his shrine. To their credit be it spoken, Mr. Spurgeon receives no countenance or encouragement from the ornaments of his denomination. He is a nine days' wonder, a comet that has suddenly shot across the religious atmosphere. He has gone up like a rocket, and ere long will come down like a stick.

In similar fashion had men spoken of Spurgeon's great Master, but he knew that this was all part of the sufferings of the disciple for the Gospel's sake, and that it would bring him blessedly close to his Lord in "the fellowship of His sufferings." The malicious critic reported above was almost wholly wrong. In one point, however, he was correct—Spurgeon, in his early ministry, did walk up and down the platform, looking now to one part of the congregation and now to another. But in later years he dropped this practice, possibly with the onset of gout in his feet. A nine days wonder...? In reality he was constant in the preaching of the Gospel for thirty-eight years. "He preaches *himself* ... his brain is turned...." Thus did ever the god of this world blind the eyes of those who believe not, to their own destruction.

The Illustrated Times wrote thus: "Nor is his popularity confined to London; lately we ourselves saw, on a weekday, in a remote agricultural district, long lines of people all converging to one point, and on inquiring of one of the party where they were going, received the answer, 'We're a goin' to hear Maester Spudgin, Sir.'" And the paper went on to predict that it was only a matter of time before the current of popularity will run and leave him.

Spurgeon made no reply to any of these attacks. He knew that his Master would vindicate him. But he had staunch friends and advocates who did reply. One of these was Mr. James Grant, editor of *The Morning Advertiser*, a paper that then ranked with *The Times* in importance. Of the Exeter Hall services he wrote:

It will easily be believed how great must be the popularity of this almost boyish preacher, when we mention that yesterday both morning and evening the large hall, capable of holding from four-thousand to five-thousand people, was filled in every part. There can be no doubt that Mr. Spurgeon possesses superior talents, while in some of his happier flights he rises to a high order of pulpit oratory. It is in pathos that he excels, though he does not himself seem to be aware of that fact. He is quite an original preacher; has evidently made George Whitefield his model; and like that unparalleled preacher, the prince of pulpit orators, is very fond of striking apostrophes.

In an article the following year, Mr. Grant instructed the readers of *The Morning Advertiser* thus:

> Never since the days of George Whitefield has any minister of religion acquired so great a reputation as this Baptist preacher, in so short a time. Here is a mere youth, a perfect stripling, only twenty-one years of age, incomparably the most popular preacher of the day. There is no man within Her Majesty's dominions who could draw such immense audiences; and none who, in his happier efforts, can so completely enthrall the attention, and delight the minds of his hearers. Some of his appeals to the conscience, some of his remonstrances with the careless, constitute specimens of a very high order of oratorical power. When pronouncing the doom of those who live and die in a state of impenitence, he makes the vast congregation quake and quail in their seats. He places their awful destiny in such vivid colors before their eyes that they almost imagine they are already in the regions of darkness and despair.

The comparison with George Whitefield is significant and just. "My own model," Spurgeon once said, "if I may have such a thing in due subordination to my Lord, is George Whitefield." And he added, with characteristic modesty, "But with unequal footsteps must I follow in his glorious track." One hardly dares to contradict Spurgeon in anything, but on this point a denial is called for. Far from following Whitefield "with unequal footsteps," he pressed on along the same path with complete success. He upheld the same Savior, preached the self-same doctrines of grace, sought to snatch guilty sinners from their awful destiny, threw himself into the Gospel battle, as Whitefield did, with thoroughgoing intensity and unwearied diligence.

The repair money at New Park Street was wasted. When the chapel was reopened, the overcrowding was worse than ever, halls, passages, side rooms chock-full. Three-thousand people packed into a fifteen-hundred capacity building. And hundreds outside unable to get in. They muddled through for a year, and then in June 1856 returned to Exeter Hall for Sunday evening services. And now ... even Exeter Hall was too small! A meeting was held to consider building a new church, and a fund was started for its erection.

Someone suggested that they should hire the palatial Surrey Music Hall, capable of holding 12,000 people! Church members looked at one another in amazement. It stood in the Royal Surrey Gardens, and was used for concerts, exhibitions, and wild beast shows. (Spurgeon thought of the early Christians facing lions in the arena at Rome!) Some thought that it would be too large; others, that a place of worldly amusements was unsuitable for Gospel preaching. The hall was taken, however, and the news of this bold scheme ran through London like wildfire. There were also more attacks in the press.

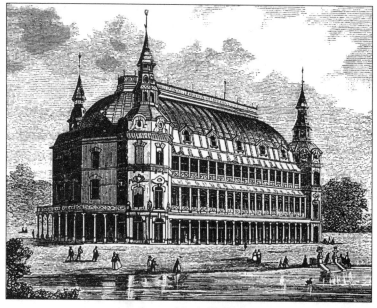

Surrey Music Hall

The first service in the Surrey Music Hall was arranged for the evening of October 19, 1856, and the streets were packed with people. It was estimated that 12,000 people were inside the vast hall, and 10,000 outside unable to get in. When Spurgeon saw the immense throng he was almost overwhelmed, but soon recovered his poise. As the hall was full the service began before the appointed time. A few words of greeting, a prayer, a hymn, and a Scripture reading. Then, as Spurgeon began another prayer, there was a commotion. Someone shouted

"FIRE!" And then: "The galleries are giving way, the place is falling!" The people rushed panic-stricken to the doors, and the young preacher tried to pacify them in vain. It was almost certainly a dastardly attempt by the servants of the devil to oppose the work of the Gospel, and it succeeded only too well. The terrified crowds stumbled and fell on the staircase, piled on top of one another; the balustrades were broken and many toppled over. It was a disaster. Seven persons lost their lives, twenty-eight were seriously injured and taken to the hospital, and many more were hurt.

Spurgeon was ignorant of the extent of the tragedy and endeavored to preach on the text "The curse of the Lord is upon the house of the wicked, but He blesseth the habitation of the just" (Proverbs 3:33). But there was a renewed disturbance, obviously from evil-disposed persons, and after a hymn was sung the meeting was brought to a close. Spurgeon was carried fainting from the pulpit, and the next day, stunned and dejected, went to a friend's house at Croydon where he might escape from the press and recover his mental balance in quietness. He spent hours in "tears by day and dreams of terror by night." One day, however, walking in his friend's garden, a message of comfort came unbidden to his heart concerning his Master—"Wherefore God has highly exalted Him, and given Him a name that is above every name." Straight-away the depression lifted and he was strengthened.

But he was slandered and vilified by almost the entire press. Of course the tragedy was all his fault. He was entirely responsible and should be hounded out of decent society. *The Saturday Review* and other papers held Spurgeon up as a vile impostor and danger to society:

"This man," it asserted, "in his opinion is a righteous Christian, but in ours nothing more than a ranting charlatan. We are neither strait-laced nor Sabbatarian[15] in our sentiments"—(no one supposed they were!)—"but we would keep apart, widely apart, the theater and the church. Above all, we would place in the hand of every thinking man a whip to scourge from society the authors of such vile blasphemies as on Sunday night, above the cries of the dead and dying, and louder than the wails of misery from the maimed and suffering, resounded from

---

15. A person who observes the seventh day of the week, Saturday, as the Sabbath or Day of Rest (worship).

the mouth of Mr. Spurgeon in the Music Hall of the Surrey Gardens."

The English of this attack is not very clear, the malice is clear enough, and fortunately for society it is pleasant to recall that *The Saturday Review* was driven to extinction in God's good time. During this time of violent and unreasoning attack, Mrs. Spurgeon had a text in bold lettering hung on their bedroom wall where every morning he would see it.

"Blessed are ye when men shall revile you, and persecute you, and shall say all manner of evil against you falsely, for My sake. Rejoice and be exceeding glad: for great is your reward in Heaven, for so persecuted they the prophets which were before you" (Mark 5:11,12).

In two weeks' time Spurgeon had recovered sufficiently to resume his ministry. This time, however, for the sake of prudence, the Surrey Music Hall was used for the morning services only. But the disaster had increased the crowds. C. H. Spurgeon had become a world figure overnight. This arrangement continued from November 23, 1856, to December 1859, when the newly-built Metropolitan Tabernacle was ready for use.

Thirty years later, on January 14, 1888, a writer in *The Daily Telegraph* commented on the accident:

> Curiously enough it was an accident of a serious nature that first drew the attention of the world in general to the rising influence of Mr. Spurgeon. The young preacher—he was then very young—had already secured an immense following on the south side of London. But the world on the other side, the world north of the Thames, the world of society and of the clubs and the West End, the world of Bloomsbury and Fitzroy Square, the world of Maida Vale and Highgate, all these various microcosms knew little or nothing of the powerful young preacher whose congregations had already far outgrown the capacity of New Park Street Chapel in Southwark. But when the accident happened, Spurgeon became famous at once. Society went out of its way, put itself to trouble to hear the young preacher whose admirers could not be contained in a building of less size than the Great Music Hall.

> Mr. Spurgeon, of course, would have been known to the whole public of these countries in time, even if there had never been a panic and a rush and a catastrophe in the Surrey Music Hall. But he found himself famous the morning after the accident, and he kept his fame. Naturally he met with some severe and scornful criticism.... As a pulpit

orator he had some special advantages. He had a voice of marvelous power, penetration, and variety of tone.... He had resources, readily drawn upon, of pathos and a certain kind of humor; and he could vivify his sermons by all manner of telling and homely, sometimes perhaps too homely, illustrations. He never preached over his listeners or at them. He always talked directly to them. He was always intensely in earnest. His emotions carried himself, as well as his congregation, away.

The qualities by which Mr. Spurgeon secured his influence have ever since enabled him to keep it, and broaden it, and deepen it.

For three years the Surrey Music Hall services continued with great success and manifest blessing, and the current of public opinion gradually changed. Tickets of admission were issued for the services in order to keep out individuals bent on mischief. One service in 1857 is described by an eye-witness as follows:

> Every seat was occupied by half-past ten o'clock, when the doors were opened to the public, then there was a rush of excited and hurried people, and in ten minutes every inch of standing room was occupied. Dr. Livingstone sat on the platform, and the Princess Royal as well as the Duchess of Sutherland were said to be present.

Other leaders of Society who went to hear Spurgeon were the Lord Chief Justice Campbell, the Lord Mayor and Sheriffs of London, Earl Russell, Lord Alfred Paget, Lord Panmure, Earl Grey, the Earl of Shaftesbury, the Marquis of Westminster, Lord Carlisle, the Earl of Elgin, Baron Bramwell, Lady Rothschild and Miss Florence Nightingale. All classes of folk went to sit at his feet and hear the Word of God. Statesmen, soldiers, authors, artists, captains of industry, farmers, peddlers, clerks, factory workers, shopkeepers, thieves, prostitutes, ne'er-do-wells and drunks. The costermongers,[16] whose livelihood depended on powerful lungs, said of him: "I never! Stunnin'! Wot a woice! Would make a good coster! ! !"

In the famous *Greville Memoirs*, Charles Cavendish Fulke Greville, the diarist, gives a personal account of Spurgeon at this period. The date is February 8, 1857:

---

16. Originally an apple peddler who sold *costards* (a variety of large apples native to England); the term came to mean a person who sells fruit or vegetables from a cart or street stand—also known as a *coster*.

I have just come from hearing the celebrated Mr. Spurgeon. He is certainly very remarkable, and undeniably a fine character; not remarkable in person; in face resembling a smaller Macaulay[17]; a very clear and powerful voice which was heard through the hall; a manner natural, impassioned, and without affectation or extravagance; wonderful fluency and command of language, abounding in illustration, and very often of a familiar kind, but without anything ridiculous or irreverent. He preached for about three-quarters of an hour, and to judge by the use of handkerchiefs and the audible sobs, with great effect.

Dr. John Tulloch, the Scottish theologian, Principal of St. Mary's College, St. Andrews, went to hear Spurgeon at the Surrey Music Hall in May 1858, in company with Professor Ferrier, the metaphysician. Dr.Tulloch wrote:

We have just been to hear Spurgeon and have both been so much impressed that I wish to give you my impressions while they are fresh. As we came out we both confessed, "There is no doubt about *that*," and I was struck with Ferrier's remarkable expression, "I feel it would do me good to hear the like of that, it sat so close to reality."

The sermon is about the most real thing I have come in contact with for a long while. Guthrie[18] is as sounding brass and a tinkling cymbal to it; and although there is not the elevated thought and descriptive facility of Caird[19] (the latter especially, however, not wanting), there is more power. Power, in fact, and life are its characteristics, and I could not help being pleased that I had hit upon the man pretty well in the notice of him along with Robertson[20] and Guthrie, which was never published.

The place is fully adapted for preaching, being the largest, lightest, and airiest building I ever saw. It was crammed, of course, but not in the least uncomfortable, as round all the thickly-studded benches there was a wide and open corridor, with window doors open, out and in of which you could walk into the Surrey Gardens as you liked; and Ferrier kept taking a turn now and then during the sermon. (Was the metaphysician's seat hard, or the sermon too long?) He began the ser-

---

17. This refers to Thomas Babington Macaulay (1800-1859) who was an English historian, author, and statesman.

18. Thomas Guthrie was a renowned evangelical preacher from Scotland.

19. Edward Caird (1835-1908) was a Scottish philosopher and theologian.

20. F. W. Robertson of Brighton was a eminent liberal preacher of the time.

vice with a short prayer, then sang the twenty-third Psalm, but instead of our fine old version, some vile version, in which the simple beauty of the hymn is entirely lost. Then he read and expounded the thirty-second chapter of Numbers. His remarks were very good and to the point, with no display or misplaced emotion. He then prayed more at length, and this was the part of the service I least liked.

He preached from the same chapter he read, about the spies in the land of Canaan—the good and bad spies. It was a parable, he said, of religion. Canaan is not rightly taken as a type of heaven, but of the religious life. Then, after speaking of men of the world judging religion, which they had no right to do, he said he would speak of two classes of people, the bad spies first, those who made a great ado about religion and did not show its power, and then the good spies. His description here was graphic beyond what I can give you an idea of, the most telling satire, cutting home, yet not overdone, as he spoke of the gloomy religionist who brought up a bad report of the land of religion, making himself and his wife and children miserable, drawing down the blinds on a Sunday, "commonly most religious when most miserable, and most miserable when most religious"; then the meek-faced fellow who can pray all Sunday and preach by the hour, and cheat all Monday, always ready with his prayer book, but keeping a singular cashbook, wouldn't swear, but would cheat and lie.

Then, again, he showed still higher powers of pathos in describing the good spies: the blind old saint who had served God for fifty years and never found Him fail; the consumptive girl testifying of the goodness of her Savior as the dews of death gathered on her brow. And then of all who only lived as Christians: the good wife who converted her husband by her untiring gentleness, and having supper ready even at twelve o'clock at night; the servant who, because she was religious cleaned knives better without losing their edge; the Christian merchant; the wife who, unknown to fame, and having no time for teaching or district visiting, achieved her household work day by day.

In fact, the whole was a wonderful display of mental vigor and Christian sense, and gave me a great idea of what good such a man can do.... He improves in look, too, a little, as he warms in preaching. At first he certainly is not interesting in face or figure—very fat and pudgy; but there is no doubt of the fellow, look as he may. His voice is of rare felicity, as clear as a bell, not a syllable lost.

In Spurgeon's twenty-third year a Day of National Humiliation was held on account of the Indian Mutiny. On October 7, 1857, Spurgeon preached in the Crystal Palace to a vast congregation of 23,654 persons counted in at the turnstiles, and up to that day considered "the largest congregation ever addressed by a preacher of the Gospel in Europe or the world." (Whitefield, be it remembered, often had 20,000 persons on Kennington Common in the early hours of morning.) Special trains were run for people to hear him. The collection, for dependents of the victims of the disaster, amounted to £675. Mrs. Spurgeon had taken her place near the front; her thoughts, no doubt, full of their courtship days. But when her Tirshatha appeared on the platform, he sent a deacon to ask her to move to a place where he could not see her, as the sight of her made him nervous! Meekly she moved to another place. Spurgeon preached a powerful sermon on the text, "Hear ye the rod, and Who hath appointed it" (Micah 6:9), full of the divine sovereignty, and of the divine grace.

Another incident connected with this great day is worth recalling. A few days previously Spurgeon went to the Crystal Palace to test the acoustics. Standing on the platform he lifted up his voice like a silver trumpet and cried, "Behold, the Lamb of God that taketh away the sin of the world." A workman, busy painting high up in one of the galleries, heard the words which seemed to come to him from heaven. In deep conviction of sin he went home, and did not rest until he was able to rejoice that Christ was his Savior. Although Spurgeon was not conscious of any extraordinary strain on the occasion of this mammoth service at the Crystal Palace, it is on record that after it was over he slept from Wednesday night until Friday morning.

The membership of the New Park Street Church grew mightily. When he came in 1854 it was 232. By January 1855 it had risen to 313. In 1855 itself there was a net increase of 282, and in 1856 an increase of 265, bringing the total to 860. In the first ten years Spurgeon baptized by immersion no less than 3,569 believers. By 1875 the membership was 4,417, and at his death in 1892 it stood at 5,307. During his entire pastorate a total of 14,700 was added; 10,800 by baptism, the rest by transfer from other churches. The growth was truly phenomenal. Thus does the Holy Spirit use those who are wholly devoted to His truth and ways.

The last service in the Surrey Music Hall was on December 11, 1859. He preached from the text, "I am pure from the blood of all men" (Acts 20:26). His voice thrilled with intensity as he called men and women to

Christ:

> In God's name, I beseech you, flee to Christ for refuge. Shall there be any of you, whom I shall see on my death-bed, who shall charge me with being unfaithful? Shall these eyes be haunted with visions of men whom I have amused, but into whose heart I have never sought to convey the truth? Shall I lie there, and shall these mighty congregations in dreary panorama before me, and as they subside, shall each one curse me as being unfaithful? God avert that worst of ills—unfaithfulness—from my head. I pray you, in Christ's stead, be ye reconciled to God!

Spurgeon preaching in Hackney Fields

During those early London years it was no uncommon thing for Spurgeon to preach ten or twelve times a week, and always to large crowds. That he stood the strain so well speaks of a very strong constitution. In September 1855 he preached in an open field in King Edward's Road, Hackney (no open fields there now, alas), to at least ten thousand people. The text was Matthew 8:11-12, and most earnestly did he urge them to flee from the wrath to come. Long was this meeting remembered; the vast sea of faces upturned to the young preacher, moving them to smile one minute, then to sobs of contrition the next as he spoke of the raptures of heaven, and the terrors of hell. Many were converted that day.

He paid his first visit to Scotland in 1855, and great throngs gathered to hear him, especially in Glasgow and Edinburgh. This Scottish visit made Spurgeon a general favorite with spiritually-minded believers there, and it is recorded that his published sermons were read more regularly there than anywhere else. A traveler relates that, getting lost in a highland glen, he found that people knew nothing about Gladstone[21] or Disraeli[22] but woke up at the name of Spurgeon. There was no *kirk* (church) in the glen, and they just met together in somebody's cottage and read one of Spurgeon's sermons. It was thus that William Robertson Nicoll came first under the influence of Spurgeon's sermons. Finding himself short of books in his first Highland parish, he discovered that a shoemaker in the village had a set of Spurgeon's sermons, and he set himself to read them all. The result was that he not only became a warm admirer of the great preacher, but also an authority on the sermons.

In the summer of 1858 Spurgeon visited Ireland, and preached four times in Belfast with great effect. It is not without significance that in the following year, 1859, the great Irish Revival began. He preached also in Dublin where, years afterwards, his grandson was to be Principal of a Baptist College. In February 1860 he paid a brief visit to Paris and preached three times in the American chapel, and at Passy. In July 1860, he was in Switzerland and preached twice in Calvin's pulpit at Geneva, and even wore Calvin's gown, a very thrilling experience for this unashamed Calvinist. April 1863 saw him in Holland, where he preached in the chief cities, sometimes for two hours at a time, with great blessing. He also visited the Queen of Holland and had a long spiritual conversation with her.

In England, wherever he was announced to preach the thousands gathered. Thousands at Parker's Piece in Cambridge, the students expecting fun strangely subdued. Thousands under the famous Cheddar Cliffs in Somerset, reminiscent of Augustus Toplady's famous hymn, "Rock of Ages Cleft for Me," which was sung. Thousands at Trowbridge, at Bristol, at Risca in South Wales. Six thousand in a wooden structure erected at Halifax, Yorkshire, which collapsed under a weight of snow three hours after he had preached there. Thousands more at Bradford, Leeds, Birmingham, Wolverhampton, Manchester,

---

21. William Ewart Gladstone (1809-1898) was a British statesman who was prime minister four times between 1868 and 1894.

22. Benjamin Disraeli (1804-1881) was a British statesman and novelist, and was prime minister in 1867 and from 1874 to 1880.

Stockon-on-Tees, Liverpool, Cheltenham, and again in Edinburgh and Aberdeen. A service on Clapham Common near his home was held in July 1859. Two weeks earlier a man sheltering beneath a tree had been killed by lightning. Ten thousand people gathered to hear Spurgeon preach on the words, "Be ye therefore also ready" (Luke 12:40), and a large collection was taken for the widow. On another occasion he preached two sermons from the grandstand of Epsom racecourse in aid of a chapel at Epsom.

In 1859 Spurgeon was offered £10,000 to go and preach sermons in New York, but they did not know their man. He preferred to go unfettered by the offer of money, and refused. His sermons were published in the United States and had a large sale, but it was noticed that all his references to the antislavery controversy were expurgated, and when he strongly denounced slavery, as he did many times, the circulation dropped greatly, particularly in the Southern States.

Spurgeon also delivered a number of lectures in various places. He spoke on such subjects as "A Christian's Pleasures," "Shrews and How to Tame Them," "Eminent Lord Mayors," "Southwark," "The Two Wesleys," "Eccentric Preachers," and several on Natural History. One of the most famous of the lectures, often repeated, was on "Sermons in Candles," when he had on a table before him candles of all shapes and sizes and colors. Another on "George Fox" he gave at the Friends' Institute, Bishopsgate, and was attended by Matthew Arnold, Lord Houghton (Monckton Milnes), and John Bright, each of whom expressed his hearty appreciation to the lecturer afterwards. He kept their interest for more than an hour and a half. It is a pity that these lectures have been forgotten and allowed to go into oblivion.

Much of this itinerant ministry and many of the lectures were given in connection with the appeal for funds for the building of the new Metropolitan Tabernacle, and in many places large sums were forthcoming.

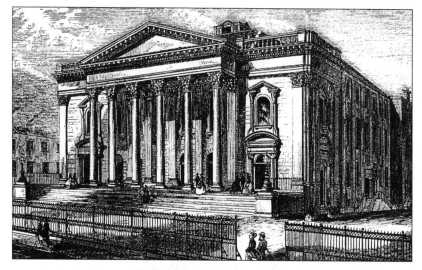

The Metropolitan Tabernacle

Chapter 6
The Metropolitan
Tabernacle

God hath but three things dear unto Him in this world, His saints,
His worship, and His truth; and it is hard to say which of these is
dearest unto Him.

—THOMAS GOODWIN, *ZERUBBABEL'S ENCOURAGEMENT*

It has already been noted that a church meeting to inaugurate a fund
for building a new and larger church was held in 1856, only two years
after he had commenced his London ministry. The need was obvious.
The Pastor, the deacons, and the whole congregation set themselves
under the good hand of God to see it built. But they were determined
on two things—the Lord would supply the great sum of money
needed, in answer to prayer; and they would on no account run into
debt. Various methods of raising money were discussed. Collectors
were appointed to gather promised gifts week by week, some quite
small amounts. A bazaar was to be held, at which some eyebrows were
raised, but Susannah was to be the leading figure in this, and all was
very decorous (there were no side shows), and it brought in £1,200. But
they were very strict on the rule that no worldly methods were to be
employed, no theatricals, no minstrel shows. The money must be
raised in a manner worthy of the Lord of Hosts, and of the Gospel of
Grace to be preached in His house.

At the initial meeting a sum of £12,000 or £15,000 was considered
sufficient for the new church, which was already being spoken of as

"the largest chapel in the world." Even this sum seemed immense for the people to raise. The Metropolitan Tabernacle actually cost £31,322, of which Spurgeon himself contributed over £5,000, and every penny was raised before the great building was opened for public worship.

It was not easy to determine the best place to build. Should it be erected at Holloway, or at Clapham, or at Kensington? Where could the most suitable land be found? Which was the neediest place for Gospel preaching? Long and anxious were the discussions on these and kindred topics. At length, some land at Newington Butts, owned by the Fishmongers' Company was brought to their notice. Spurgeon felt that as they were fishers of men it would be most suitable! There was a fine frontage near Elephant and Castle, where several roads converged. There was sufficient ground available, and it was easy to access. In addition, and most significant in Spurgeon's eyes, three Anabaptists had been burned nearby in the reign of Popish Mary. The only hindrance might be that there was already a Baptist Chapel in the very next street. (The good friends there were naturally alarmed, and when the matter was discussed, refused to amalgamate with Spurgeon's congregation, and continued their own cause.) Unfortunately, the land was in an estate held by lease, but through the providential intervention of an influential Member of Parliament, the purchase of the land was arranged to be held for life, although a special Act of Parliament was needed to transfer it to the church.

The question of what manner of building it should be arose at the outset and was warmly debated. Architects were invited to submit plans, and prizes were offered for the most suitable. No less than sixty-two sets of drawings, and one model, were sent in by January 1859. The design that was awarded the first prize was not accepted, but the eighth on the list which was given the second prize, eventually adopted. The architect was W. W. Pocock. It was a Grecian-style building, with six massive Corinthian columns forming an imposing porch in front. Spurgeon was resolutely opposed to Gothic architecture. At the foundation-stone laying ceremony on August 16, 1859, he said:

> It is a matter of congratulation to me that in this city we should build a Grecian place of worship. There are two sacred languages in the world, the Hebrew of old, and the Greek that is dear to every Christian heart. The standard of our faith is Greek, and this place is to be Grecian. Greek is the sacred tongue, and Greek is the Baptist's tongue. We may

be beaten in our own version sometimes, but in the Greek never. Every Baptist place should be Greek, never Gothic.

Years later he wrote in his autobiography, "Long ago I made up my mind that either a suitable place must be built or I would resign my pastorate.... I sternly resolved that one or other must be done—either the Tabernacle must be erected, or I would become an Evangelist, and turn rural dean of all the commons in England, and vicar of all the hedgerows." It is fascinating to speculate what would have been the effect on the nation if Charles Haddon Spurgeon had become another itinerant George Whitefield.

The foundation stone was laid by Sir Samuel Morton Peto, MP,[23] a distinguished Baptist layman of the time and a railway magnate. Beneath it was placed a Bible, the Baptist Confession of Faith, Dr. Rippon's Hymn-book, and a statement by the deacons of the church, which has already been quoted. An invalid at Bristol sent £3,000 to be laid on the stone, with a challenge that if twenty others gave £100 each, he would add another £2,000 to match theirs. They did ... and he did!

The Metropolitan Tabernacle was dignified, comfortable, spacious, seating 5,000 people. The building was 174 feet in length, 81 feet broad, and 62 feet high. It had two galleries, one above the other, a large schoolroom seating 900 beneath the chapel, a large rostrum for the preacher, but no organ and no choir. (An organ was added after Spurgeon's day.) The singing was led by a man with a tuning fork! Musical accompaniments were regarded as unseemly in those days. But the singing was hearty and inspiring. Later, Spurgeon compiled his own hymnbook of a strong Calvinist flavor.

The building contractor was William Higgs, one of his deacons, a businessman of a radiant Christian character, entirely self-effacing. Concerning Mr. Higgs, Spurgeon said:

Eternity alone can reveal all the generous feeling and self-denying liberality evinced by Christian people in connection with the enterprise—to us, at any rate, so gigantic at the time that, apart from Divine aid, we could never have carried it through. One of the chief of our mercies was the fact that our beloved brother William Higgs was our

---

23. This abbreviation refers to a person who is a "Member of Parliament." Parliament is the chief legislative body of Great Britain, consisting of the House of Lords and the House of Commons.

builder, and treated us with unbounded liberality throughout the whole affair."

The New Park Street property was finally to be auctioned when it was found impractical to carry on a mission there. Higgs, without saying anything to anybody, privately bid it in, sold it a few days later at a profit of £800, and then brought the entire sum and laid it on Spurgeon's desk as a gift to God.

One evening after the builders had left the site, Spurgeon encountered the secretary of the Building Committee "having a look round" like himself. When they had walked about a little, Spurgeon suggested that they should seek God's blessing on the work. So, in the gathering dusk, and with piles of bricks and stacks of timber all around, they committed the building and the men engaged on it to God's care. There was not a single serious accident during the whole process of the building.

Spurgeon named the new church "The Metropolitan Tabernacle" after the great Tent of Meeting of the wilderness wanderings of Israel. The Christian life was a pilgrim life; earth was their lodge, and Heaven their home. It was set up, in all its immensity, to the glory of God, and for the blessing and salvation of souls. At the beginning of his sixth year in London, at the age of only twenty-five, he saw God's hand put forth to establish their great new House of God, which was to be thronged with thousands upon thousands of seeking souls and convinced believers for the succeeding thirty-one years of his ministry—an average of 5,000 people every Sunday morning and evening.

The opening service of the Metropolitan Tabernacle was held on Monday afternoon, March 25, 1861. With what enthusiasm and delight the people thronged in to behold their splendid new church. Spurgeon preached to a crowded congregation on the text, "And daily in the Temple, and in every house, they ceased not to teach and to preach Jesus Christ" (Acts 5:42). (With what felicity did he choose his texts on such great occasions.) In the course of his address he said:

> I would propose (and O may the Lord grant me grace to carry out that proposition) that the subject of the ministry of this house, as long as this platform shall stand, and as long as this house shall be frequented by worshippers, shall be the person of Jesus Christ. I am never ashamed to avow myself a Calvinist, although I claim to be rather a Calvinist according to Calvin, than after the modern debased fashion.

I do not hesitate to take the name of Baptist ... but if I am asked to say what is my creed, I think I must reply: "It is Jesus Christ." My venerated predecessor, Dr. Gill, has left a body of divinity, admirable and excellent in its way, but the body of divinity to which I would pin and bind myself for ever, God helping me, is not his system of divinity, or any other human treatise, but Christ Jesus, Who is the sum and substance of the Gospel; Who is in Himself all theology, the incarnation of every precious truth, the all-glorious personal embodiment of the way, the truth, and the life.

He went on to commend the Lord Jesus Christ in His infinite and indisputable Godhead, His true humanity, as the only Mediator between God and man, in the solitariness of His redemptive work, as the only Law-giver of the Church, as the sole king of the Church, and as the King of Kings. Spurgeon declared:

If I preach Christ, I must preach Him as the covenant head of His people, and how far am I then from the doctrine of election? If I preach Christ, I must preach the efficacy of His blood, and how far am I then removed from the great doctrine of an effectual atonement? If I preach Christ, I *must* preach the love of His heart, and how can I deny the final perseverance of the saints? If I preach the Lord Jesus as the great Head and King, how far am I removed from Divine Sovereignty? Must I not, if I preach Christ personally, preach His doctrines? I believe they are nothing but the natural outgrowth of that great root thought, or root substance rather, the person of the Lord Jesus Christ.... Of every virtue He is the pattern; of the perfection of human character, He is the very mirror; of everything that is holy and of good report, He is the abiding incarnation.

Thus he nailed his colors to the mast. And he concluded thus:

May I entreat in closing, your earnest prayer, each one of you, that in this house as well as in all the places of worship round about, Christ may ever more be preached; and I may add my own sincere desire that this place may become a hissing and an abode of dragons, and this pulpit be burned with fire, if ever any other gospel be preached here than that which we have received of the holy Apostle of God, and of which Jesus Christ Himself is the chief Cornerstone. May I claim your earnest and constant intercessions, that where Christ is lifted up, men may be drawn to hear, and afterwards drawn to believe, that they may find Christ the Savior of our souls.

There was no doubt about *that*, as Principal Tulloch would have said!

In the evening Dr. W. Brock preached on the words, "Christ is preached, and I therein do rejoice, yea and will rejoice" (Philippians 1:18). For three weeks the opening services and meetings continued, and a spate of evangelical oratory poured forth. Long meetings, and long sermons too. There were meetings for the contributors, for the neighboring churches, for the Baptists of London, for the various other denominations, for the Tabernacle church members, and for the Baptist Missionary Society. On Good Friday Spurgeon preached twice, and announced that all the money needed had been given, and that the Tabernacle was opened free of debt. On one evening Dr. Octavius Winslow preached on "Christ's Finished Work" (John 19:30), and on another the Rev. Hugh Stowell Brown preached on "Christian Baptism" (Colossians 2:12). Henry Vincent delivered what was described as "An Oration" on Nonconformity, a tremendous historical review, with General Sir John Burgo, GCB,[24] in the chair.

Then there was a series of expositions of the doctrines of grace, in which the "five points of Calvinism" were set forth at length: "Election," by the Rev. John Bloomfield; "Human Depravity," by the Rev. Evan Probert; "Particular Redemption," by his brother the Rev. James A. Spurgeon; "Effectual Calling," by the Rev. James Smith: and "The Final Perseverance of Believers in Christ Jesus," by the Rev. William O'Neill.

The trumpet gave no uncertain sound. The truths of free, sovereign and distinguishing grace, the setting forth of Christ in all His preciousness and truth, the earnest calling of sinners to come to the Savior, the declaration of the whole counsel of God as set forth in the inspired Scriptures—these were the mighty themes for which the great church was built, and these the themes Spurgeon delighted to preach for over thirty years. Not only on Sundays was the Tabernacle filled, but on Thursday evenings also the congregation often overflowed into the top gallery. "How many thousand have been converted here," he exclaimed at the Prayer Meeting on May 26, 1890. "There has not been a single day but what I have heard of two, three or four having been converted; and that not for one, two or three years, but for the last ten years." Mighty were the Prayer Meetings held on Monday nights, when the

---

24. This abbreviation refers to the "Grand Cross of the Bath"—a high honor bestowed upon a British citizen by a patron such as the ruling monarch—and signifies that the individual is an exclusive member of the Order of the Bath.

large number of praying people felt the power of the Holy Spirit in their midst.

The members of the Church were provided with tickets in order that they might secure a seat. The general public had to queue up and take a chance of finding a place when they were admitted five minutes before the service started. The newcomer to the Tabernacle was often surprised at the buzz of conversation which preceded the entry of the preacher, or at the reading of newspapers on the part of some. It seemed more like a concert hall than a place of worship. All was changed, however, when Spurgeon appeared, and a reverent hush fell over the vast throng.

Inside the Metropolitan Tabernacle

The flaps along the aisles at the pew ends were let down and occupied; the gangways in the galleries were packed; the vast oval-shaped auditorium was crammed with people from the floor to the back of the top gallery. Yet all was practical and businesslike in the arrangements. The stewardship was superb. The Tabernacle was light, the color-scheme cheerful, the seats comfortable and commodious. The acoustics were perfect. The whole place was designed that the congregation might sit in comfort, and hear and see without strain.

Printed papers giving the hymn numbers, and a word of exhortation to all about singing were found on every seat. "It is earnestly requested that every sincere worshipper will endeavor to join in the song, carefully attending to time and tune, and above all being concerned to worship the Lord in spirit and in truth." On hot Sundays these papers provided convenient fans for perspiring hearers.

At the hour of eleven, or six-thirty, punctual to a second, a door in the back platform opened, and a stout, plain man with a familiar face advanced to the table on the platform which protruded into the well of the auditorium and was clearly visible from all sides. Upon it stood a table, chair and sofa. On the table rested a Bible. Spurgeon was followed by a dozen deacons who sat immediately behind their minister. Having spent a few moments in prayer, he gazed round on the great congregation. Then he rose, raised his hand above his head, and the service opened with prayer. Immediately a fresh hush fell upon the assembly. A hymn followed, Spurgeon announcing it slowly and with enormous distinctness. A precentor[25] stepped forward on the lower platform and started a familiar tune, which the whole congregation of 5-6,000 took up in all its harmonies, but in perfect time and expression. The praise at the Tabernacle was one of the most delightful and unforgettable things.

The reading of Scripture followed, and this was apt to be a lengthy business because Spurgeon would give a shrewd, earnest, running commentary on each verse of the passage as he read it. Many of his finest thoughts, based on his reading of the Puritans, came out in these Scripture readings. Dr. James Denney, the theologian, wrote to tell Sir William Robertson Nicoll how he had been to the Tabernacle to hear Spurgeon, and how impressed he was at Spurgeon's reading of Scripture:

> I once heard him read the third chapter of Daniel, about the burning, fiery furnace, etc. He read it a little pompously, all about the harp, lyre, psaltery, etc., down to verse 7, "the golden image that Nebuchadnezzar the king had set up." Then he made a little pause, and said with ironical emphasis on the last word, "Church and State." Then he read on to the end where Nebuchadnezzar makes the contrary decree appointing the fiery furnace for all who speak against the God of the Hebrew chil-

---

25. The precentor is a person who leads in congregation singing. This role was of particular importance to the Puritans since they disapproved of anything that was ostentatious (i.e., the use of musical instruments in public worship).

dren, and after another little pause with created expectation, he said, "Church and State again—and *wrong every time.*"

Another hymn, and then a second prayer. Spurgeon disliked his prayers being reported, but many were, and a volume was published under the title, *The Pastor in Prayer,* a rare treasure indeed. The anointing from the Holy One was upon him when he prayed. There was a combination of awe, richness, spontaneity, devotion, directness, and practicality which made an abiding impression. Here was a man who had come, one felt, out of the audience chamber of the Most High.

The most remarkable part of the whole service was, of course, the sermon. With masterly skill he opened up his text, well divided his subject into many divisions and subdivisions, as the Puritans had taught him to do; deftly dropped in a telling illustration, carefully explained a vital doctrine, carried home the argument or appeal to mind, heart, conscience, and will, with now a touch of humor, now a touch of pathos. Texts there were many, but only one subject. Christ and His truth and great Salvation was the essence of every sermon. He was truly the embodiment of the Puritan preacher in the picture which Christian saw in the Interpreter's house in *Pilgrim's Progress:* "It had eyes lift up to heaven, the best of books in his hand, the Law of Truth was written upon his lips, the World was behind his back; it stood as if it pleaded with men, and a Crown of Gold did hang over his head."

Spurgeon preached energetically too, at least in his earlier days, marching to and fro on his platform, rather like an American advocate in front of the witness' stand, gazing now at one part of his congregation, now at another. Without a doubt he overawed and gripped the vast assemblies as one man. The flow of simple Saxon speech, the rich, deep voice that penetrated to the most distant parts of the Tabernacle, the solemnity of the message as coming direct from the Lord Himself, and the homely comprehensibility of it all—attracted and held the attention, none present but realized that the Lord of Hosts was with him in very deed!

The famous preacher Dr. R. W. Dale of Carr's Lane Chapel, Birmingham, records thus, from personal experience:

While they were worshipping with him the glory of the Lord shone round about them, and this has never been to the same extent their experience in listening to any other man. Never again will they listen to a preacher at whose word God will become so near, so great, so terrible, so gracious; Christ so tender and so strong; the Divine Spirit so mighty and so merciful; the Gospel so free; the promises of God so firm; the troubles of the Christian man so light; his inheritance in Christ so glorious and so real. Never again. It is wonderful that such large numbers of Christian men should, in the Divine order, be made so dependent on one man.

There was no preaching then in England to compare with his for popular influence. He swept London like a tornado. He has often been compared with George Whitefield, but the comparison seems futile, for their spheres of labor were so different. Whitefield, like Wesley, took the whole world for his parish, while Spurgeon restricted himself for the most part to a single pulpit. He was in the front rank of masters of the Christian pulpit. And how Whitefield would have delighted in his preaching and hung upon his words, they were so full of Christ, and so faithful to the Gospel.

One has looked into a number of contemporary Anglican biographies for any allusions to Spurgeon and his marvelous ministry. Most of them ignore him altogether. F. D. Maurice, writing in 1859, seemed to think that the staple of his preaching was "hell and the devil." "If," he went on, "he should waken up to the perception of a God of absolute love, his popularity would probably vanish." Which only goes to show what things may be hidden from the wise and prudent.

Spurgeon never forgot how he himself had been brought to Christ and gloriously saved, in a moment, in the little Primitive Methodist Chapel at Colchester. That initial experience lent color and shape to all his preaching. He was too wise a man to imagine that God had only one way of dealing with human souls, but he did believe that what had happened to him might happen to others. He believed that conversions like his own—swift, sudden, dramatic—were always possible. He preached for them and expected them. It was *while Peter yet spoke,* so he read in his New Testament, that the Holy Spirit fell on them. Spurgeon believed that even as he spoke lives might be changed; and they assuredly were.

Sir William Robertson Nicoll writes of Spurgeon's remarkable voice: "clear as a silver bell's, and winning as a woman's, rose up against the surging multitude, and without effort entered every ear."

The Metropolitan Tabernacle became one of the show places of London. Visitors to the city went as naturally to hear Spurgeon as they went to Westminster Abbey or the Tower of London. It was said at the time that the vast majority of Americans who crossed the Atlantic had two chief desires—one was to visit Shakespeare's Stratford-upon-Avon, and the other to listen to Charles Haddon Spurgeon at the Metropolitan Tabernacle.

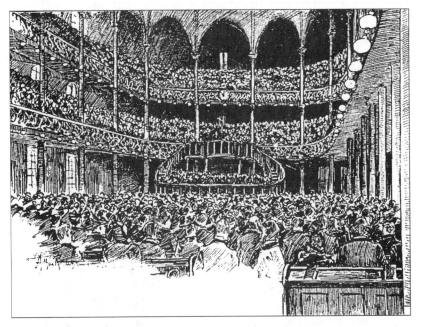

The Metropolitan Tabernacle filled with listeners

On January 8, 1882, the Prime Minister, Mr. W. E. Gladstone, accompanied by his son, visited the Tabernacle. They spent a little time with Spurgeon in the vestry before the service, and occupied a pew immediately behind the platform. The text that evening was Mark 5:30, "Who touched My clothes?" and the Prince of Preachers gave a simple Gospel sermon. The great Liberal statesman listened with evident enjoyment. After the service he returned to the vestry, and was introduced to the deacons and elders, and expressed his appreciation of all he had heard and seen. It was commonly reported that Her Majesty Queen Victoria herself had visited the Tabernacle one day in disguise; it may have been so, but it is extremely unlikely.

Many great occasions were celebrated at the Tabernacle. On May 20, 1879, the Spurgeons' silver wedding anniversary brought a huge congregation who presented their Pastor with a love offering of no less a sum than £6,476, the bulk of which he gave to the almshouses connected with the church. The Jubilee meetings of his ministry were held on June 18-19, 1884, amidst great enthusiasm and rejoicing, when a sum of £4,500 was presented to him, which money he also used for the work he had inaugurated. It was said at the time that more would have been subscribed had it not been realized that he would give it all away!

The history of the Metropolitan Tabernacle after Spurgeon's time is a sad one. The vast building was burned to the ground on Wednesday, April 20, 1898, six years after Spurgeon's death. Only the famous portico and the outer walls remained. Under the ministry of his son, Thomas Spurgeon, it was rebuilt and reconstructed at a cost of £45,000 but with a smaller seating capacity. It was opened free of debt on September 19, 1900. During the ministry of the Rev. Tydeman Chilvers an organ was installed for the first time.

During the Second World War the Tabernacle was the victim of the Nazi blitz in 1941, and again almost totally destroyed. But again it was not the end. After the war the building was reconstructed and rebuilt once more, but on a smaller scale. Will it ever see crowds again? Yes, if God sends revival. But it still remains a witness and a memorial of a great ministry which has never been surpassed.

One of the many 'cartoons' made of Spurgeon. This one was from "The Hornet."

Chapter 7
The Sermons

A good book is the precious lifeblood of a master spirit, embalmed and treasured up on purpose to a life beyond life.

—JOHN MILTON

What fitter time to converse with our Lord, than on the Lord's day? What fitter day to ascend to heaven, than that on which He arose from earth, and fully triumphed over death and hell. Use your Sabbaths as steps to glory, till you have passed them all, and are there arrived.

—RICHARD BAXTER, *THE SAINTS' EVERLASTING REST*

Robert Louis Stevenson writes in one of his delightful essays of the little island of Earraid, off the West coast of Scotland, and of its Sabbath services. He mentions the singing of the Psalms, the chapters read, and "the inevitable Spurgeon's sermon." Evidently they had no minister, and the printed sermon was read and received with great appreciation.

In his life of Dr. John Watson (whose pen name was Ian Maclaren), Sir William Robertson Nicoll tells of the regular arrival at one of the Blairgowrie farms of Spurgeon's weekly sermon. The farmer setting out to market was instructed by his wife to bring home tea and sugar and oil and the other necessities of life. "And, John, dinna forget Spurgeon!" Spurgeon was the weekly number of the Metropolitan Tabernacle Pulpit, price one penny. When he returned, the good woman read the title, "The Salvation of Manasseh." "It would have been a fine-like business to have missed that," she said, "a'll warrant this 'ill be ane o' his sappiest, but they're a' gude." And Manasseh was put in a prominent place in the best parlor till the Sabbath. When Sabbath came the lads from the bunk house were brought into the kitchen and entertained to tea. Then afterwards the master of the house read a sermon by Spurgeon. That evening the gathering was held in the barn, and John Watson, then a lad, was given the honor to read Manasseh. Years later, he wrote:

> I do not know whether it was one of the greatest of Mr. Spurgeon's sermons, but it was mighty unto salvation in that barn, and I make no doubt that good grain was garnered unto eternity. There is a passage in it when, after the mercy of God has rested on this chief sinner, an angel flies through the length and breadth of Heaven crying, "Manasseh is saved, Manasseh is saved!" Up to this point I read, and further did not read....
>
> He was overcome with emotion. "Ye'll be tired, noo," said the good farmer. "Let me feenish the sermon....

Mighty unto salvation! Many have declared that, influential as his preaching was, the influence of his printed sermons was even greater.

The sermons were published weekly, every Thursday, beginning August 20, 1854, and continued without a break for a quarter of a century after his death; finally coming to an end, not with the exhaustion of the sermons, but because of paper rationing during the First World War, in May 1917. At first called the New Park Street Pulpit, and then the Metropolitan Tabernacle Pulpit, they stand on the shelves in their black calf, sixty-three volumes in all. He first conceived the idea of issuing his own sermons in pamphlet form by reading those of the Rev. Joseph Irons of Camberwell, a favorite of his.

The publication of the sermons was quite a romance in its own right. On Spurgeon's very first Sunday in London a young printer, Joseph Passmore, insisted on walking home with him to his lodgings. When Spurgeon settled at New Park Street, Mr. Passmore took a chance (though Spurgeon would have said it was just another act of Providence) on the weekly publication of Spurgeon's sermons. It was hard-going to make ends meet in the small press-room at the beginning, but Spurgeon's name, and sermons and books, at length made the firm of Passmore and Alabaster wealthy. They became deacons of the church, and an intimate fellowship grew between them.

"I am so attached to these friends," Spurgeon said, "that I have no wish to have any other publishers as long as I live; our business arrangements are such as Christian men would desire to make so that in all things God might be glorified." The three men labored together for thirty-six years, and all died within a few months of each other.

Messrs. Passmore and Alabaster issued about 5,000 sermons in all, of which it was estimated that *one hundred million* were sold. On one occasion the publishers received an order for a million copies, and on another occasion a quarter of a million were bought to be distributed to the crowned heads of Europe (more in those days than now!), Members of Parliament, and students at the universities. One gentleman valued them so highly that he paid for their weekly insertion, as advertisements, in Australian papers. An enterprising American syndicate cabled the Sunday morning sermons across the Atlantic for publication in the United States. The sermons were translated and published in French, German, Dutch, Swedish, Italian, and many other languages and he received letters concerning them, and often telling of conversions, from all parts of the world. Spurgeon became a best-seller!

At the beginning of every annual bound volume was the following majestic attribution:

TO

THE ONE GOD OF HEAVEN AND EARTH

IN

THE TRINITY OF ITS SACRED PERSONS,

BE ALL HONOUR AND GLORY,

WORLD WITHOUT END,

AMEN.

TO THE GLORIOUS FATHER, AS COVENANT GOD

OF ISRAEL;

TO THE GRACIOUS SON, REDEEMER OF HIS PEOPLE;

TO THE HOLY GHOST, THE AUTHOR OF

SANCTIFICATION;

BE EVERLASTING PRAISE FOR THAT GOSPEL OF THE

FREE GRACE OF GOD,

HEREIN PROCLAIMED UNTO MEN.

Spurgeon delighted in the ever-increasing sale of his sermons. They were used by earnest tract-distributors, read to the sick in hospital wards, taken into prisons, preached by humble laymen in pastorless chapels, pondered over by sailors at sea.

They were taken down in shorthand on delivery, and the printers' boy arrived with the proof early on Monday morning. Spurgeon then set to work to revise his message for publication. Often extensive alterations were made, though the substance of the sermon remained.

Spurgeon used gestures to bring home his message

His methods of sermon preparation were peculiarly his own, and none but a spiritual genius and an alert, Bible-steeped mind could have continued to use it year after year. Not for him the quiet study at his desk from Tuesday morning onwards. He left his pulpit preparation to Saturday evenings and Sunday afternoons! Whether he would have adopted another method had he had a college training cannot be said with certainty. But this was his well-tried method, and he succeeded with it. On Saturday afternoons he usually had friends to tea, and after tea would conduct family worship with them. But it was understood that they must leave by seven o'clock. Then he went to his study to prepare his Sunday morning sermon. Sometimes the text, subject, and outline came easily, and within an hour or two he had his notes neatly written on a half-sheet of note paper, the main points and subdivisions set out in order so that a mere glance would refresh his thoughts. At times, of course, the theme of the sermon had been pondered all the week. He strongly believed in preparing *himself* rather than the sermon, but of course his natural fluency and power to think on his feet was exceptional. On Sunday afternoons he would again retire to his study to prepare the evening sermon. But it was not all plain-sailing. He said himself:

> I confess that I frequently sit hour after hour praying and waiting for a subject, and that is the main part of my study; much hard labor have I spent in manipulating topics, making skeletons out of verses. Almost every Sunday of my life I prepare enough outlines of sermons to last me for a month, but I no more dare use them than an honest mariner would run ashore a cargo of contraband goods. Let those preach lightly who will; to me it is "the Burden of the Lord" which at times crushes my whole manhood into the dust of humiliation. I drift on and on over leagues of broken water, till I see the red lights and make sail direct to the desired haven!

Then he would consult the commentaries, and his beloved Puritans, and distill excellent matter from them for his purpose.

Not surprisingly, Spurgeon had several trying experiences on preparing his sermons in this way. One evening his mind was directed to the text, "Thy people shall be willing in the day of Thy power." But, try as he would, and although he worked late, the sermon would not come, and he was unable to construct a satisfactory outline. Tired and dejected he appeared to his wife, who advised him to go to bed, and promised to wake him early in the morning to give him time to prepare. Scarcely had he fallen asleep, however, than he began to talk in his sleep and to preach the sermon on the chosen text! Mrs. Spurgeon very carefully noted the various points as he gave them, and in the morning told him what he had preached in the night. "Why," he said, "that is just what I wanted." At the customary hour he stood in his pulpit and preached the word with power. On another occasion, driven for time, he was forced to make notes of a sermon in his carriage on the way to the evening service, but the Lord undertook for him, and the sermon was greatly blessed to many. On his travels he always had with him a notebook in which he jotted down incidents, anecdotes, and thoughts he could use as illustrations. From this notebook some of his smaller books like *Feathers for Arrows* were compiled.

Dr. E. B. Pusey, the Tractarian leader, is reported to have said, "I love the Evangelicals because of their great love for Christ." And multitudes of people of all classes loved Spurgeon for the self-same reason. Once when Samuel Rutherford was pouring out his heart on the loveliness of Christ, the Duke of Argyll cried out, "Oh man, keep on in that strain!" Spurgeon kept on in that strain, delighting to speak of the excellencies and saving grace of his Well-beloved. His theme was ever Christ and His love for the souls of men. His sermons were Christ-centered and Christ-exalting. In the preface to the 1859 volume of his sermons, Spurgeon said :

> The simple preaching of Jesus cannot fail under the hand of the Holy Spirit to produce the very best effects. No fine words are needed; no swelling periods; simplicity and earnestness will win the day. Sound doctrine and loving invitation make a good basis of material which, when modeled by the hand of prayer and faith, will form sermons of far more value in the saving of souls than the most philosophic essays, prepared elaborately, and delivered with elegance and propriety. No excuse is offered for the roughness and rusticity of the language, since this the better adapts them for humble readers; but the preacher begs the large indulgence of his brethren in Christ for the faults of which he is sorrowfully conscious, but which have not restrained the Spirit of God from working by His Word.

Again, introducing the 1861 volume he wrote:

> In the matter of Gospel doctrine, we trust no reader will perceive any variation. No new gospel have we aimed to declare. More faith is needed, but not a new creed; a firmer confidence, but not a better covenant; a stronger trust, but not a more solid foundation. Developments, discoveries, and theorizings we are content to leave to those who, having never tasted the old wine, are naturally thirsty for the new. Our colors are nailed to the mast, and in doctrine we take for our motto, *Semper idem* [Latin, "always the same"]. We are foolish enough, as the new divines would say, to be content with the old the-

ology, and even to believe it incapable of improvement. We do not think the Essays and Reviews an advance upon Paul and Peter; nor do we rank Messrs. Maurice, Kingsley, and others of the cloudy schools, with Luther and Calvin. Pestilent heresies, advocated by cunning and crafty men, who lay in wait to deceive: are endeavoring to sap the foundations of all our churches, and our only safety lies in adhering tenaciously to the old truth, and seeking a fresh baptism of the Holy Spirit, that the Life of God may be continued in our midst. "Hold fast the form of sound words."

Here, let it be noted, is a foreshadowing of the stand taken in the "Down Grade" controversy.

Dr. Andrew Murray well expresses the heart of Spurgeon's preaching. In his preface to a collection of Spurgeon's sermons entitled *Christ's Relation to His People,* he writes:

Some twenty years ago when, by the loss of my voice, I was laid aside from preaching, I was led to read carefully a volume of Spurgeon's sermons. As I read, the question came as to what might be the secret of their power. I thought I found the answer in what may be considered the keynote of all his preaching—the Name of our Blessed Redeemer as a living Person, a loving and most beloved Friend and Lord. The Lord Jesus was to him such an intense, living reality, he believed so in His nearness and presence and the wonderful love with which he loves us, that the hearer felt that he spoke out of living experience of what he had seen and heard. Very often the very sentence of a sermon opened at once the way into the presence of Christ. While many ministers speak under the impression that their hearers are low down in the plain and must slowly and gradually be led up to the inward truth of the Gospel, Mr. Spurgeon was never afraid to come forth as one who was living with his Lord in the enjoyment of his salvation and love, and as from the door of the King's palace to cry: "Enter in; He is here; fear not." In the fullest sense of the word, "he ceased not to teach and to preach Jesus Christ."

Spurgeon was an *expository* preacher *par excellence.* He preached from every book of the Bible, and from some passages many times. A study of the index of texts of any of the annual volumes will show how he drew his themes from all parts of Scripture. There are the great well-known passages such as "Enoch walking with God," Abraham's faith, Isaiah 53, Jesus the Good Shepherd, the Prodigal Son, the Raising of Lazarus, The Cross of Calvary, The Resurrection, Justification by Faith Only, Sanctification by the Spirit, the Whole Armour of God, etc., etc.

And there are unusual and strange texts and subjects, such as "Am I a Sea or a Whale?," "Abram and the Ravenous Bird," "The Shankbone Sermon," "A Sermon for the Worst Man on Earth," etc., etc.

T. E. Aug. 7. 90.   1 Chron XXVIII, 19.

    The temple must not be left to man, but built according to pattern.

     It was to be a type of mysterious truth.
     It was to be / habitation o God.
     It was to be / throne o / King.

   No man c⁰ᵈ devised it to God's mind.
     It is not even left to Solomon

I. The singular instruction o David:

    1. He held no consultation w men.
    2. He did not follow / former model
    3. The details were given
    4. Great minuteness displayed
    5. The innermost things laid bare.
    6. On his understanding these were written
    7. The hand of the Lord wrote all.

II. The spiritual tuition of saints in / pattern of truth.

    1. To us also there is hand-writing on the heart.
    2. All / great truths are so written
       Ruin, helplessness, Regeneration, Redemption &c
    3. The points o / pattern o holiness are so written.
    4. The details o salvation are so written
       The porch, the houses, the treasuries,
       The upper rooms, the parlours, / places many &c
       " Treasuries o / dedicated things

Notes for a sermon on 1 Chronicles 28:19, August 1890.

Some of the sermons were especially beloved and became quite famous. "There Go the Ships," "Looking unto Jesus," "Compel Them to Come In"—which is said to have led to the conversion of more souls than any other sermon he ever preached!—"The Shameful Sufferer," which was Susannah's favorite, "Things That Accompany Salvation," "One born Out of Due Time," "Runaway Jonah and the Convenient Ship," "Lay Hold on Eternal Life," and "Accepted in the Beloved." But perhaps the sermon on the theme, "Supposing Him to be the Gardener," is the most striking. It has been constantly reprinted, and has been blessed to many thousands. Only a few years ago it was read on BBC[26] radio in an abridged version, and the message came over the air with compelling power. How the great preacher would have delighted in this broadcast.

A leading article in *The Times* of June 19, 1884, gave testimony to the power of Spurgeon's preaching:

> Mr. Spurgeon laid his foundation in the Bible, his utterances abound with Scriptural text, figure, metaphor, and allusion. Whatever he says sends his hearers to the sacred record. But starting from this basis he has added to it a stock of reading such as few men can show in their talk or in their writing. He cannot be accused of not being a man of the world, or of not knowing the ways of the world, for he reads the Book and the book of nature too. His style is illustrated with almost pictorial brightness.... We are not sure that Latimer[27] and Ridley's sermons would not jar on modern refinement quite as much, but they never would have reformed the Church of England with smooth words and a pure classic style.

It is remarkable that although he preached thousands of sermons there was hardly any repetition. Even when dealing with the same theme the sermons are minted afresh from his deeply-taught mind and Christ-devoted heart. He once said at a Bible Society meeting:

> What a storehouse the Bible is, since a man may continue to preach from it for years and still find that there is more to preach from than when he began to discourse upon it. What pyramids of books have been written upon the Bible, and yet we who are students find no por-

---

26. This abbreviation refers to the "British Broadcasting Corporation."

27. Hugh Latimer (1485?-1555) and Nicholas Ridley (1500?-1555) were both English bishops and Protestant reformers who were burned at the stake.

tion over-expounded, but large parts which have been scarcely
touched.... I might almost say that the major part of the Word of God
is still an El Dorado[28] unexplored, a land whose dust is gold."

And he told the students of New College, London, in October 1866,
"For twelve years my sermons have been reported and printed, and yet
in my search for something new I pace up and down my study embar-
rassed with the abundance of topics, not knowing which to choose."

His preaching caught the attention and interested people partly
because of the variety of the subjects with which he dealt. He told his
students:

> I think it well to frequently look over the list of my sermons, and see
> whether any doctrine has escaped my attention, or any Christian grace
> has been neglected in my ministrations. It is well to inquire whether
> we have been too doctrinal lately, or too barely practical, or too exclu-
> sively experimental.... We would give every portion of Scripture its
> fair share in our heart and head. Doctrine, precept, history, type,
> psalm, proverb, experience, warning, promise, invitation, threatening
> or rebuke—we would include the whole of inspired truth within the
> circle of our teachings.

The well of inspiration never dried up. "Our range of subjects is all
but boundless," he said, "and we cannot therefore be excused if our discourses are threadbare and devoid of substance. If we speak as ambassadors of God, we need never complain of want of matter, for our
message is full to overflowing. The entire Gospel must be presented
from the pulpit; the whole faith once delivered to the saints must be
proclaimed by us."

Whatever text he chose he related it directly to the Lord Jesus Christ.

> Our great master theme is the good news from heaven; the tidings of
> mercy through the atoning death of Jesus, mercy to the chief of sinners
> upon their believing in Jesus.... First, and above all things keep to
> plain Evangelical doctrines; whatever else you do or do not preach, be
> sure incessantly to bring forth the soul-saving truth of Christ and Him
> crucified ... Preach Christ always and ever more. He is the whole Gos-
> pel. His person, offices, and works must be our one great, all-compre-
> hending theme. The world still needs to be told of its Savior, and of the
> way to reach Him.... Man's fall, his need of a new birth, forgiveness

---

28. A legendary treasure city for which early Spanish explorers sought, supposedly
located in South America; now refering to any fabulously wealthy place.

through an atonement and salvation as the result of faith, these are our battle-ax and weapons of war.... Salvation is a theme for which I would fain enlist every holy tongue. I am greedy after witnesses for the glorious Gospel of the blessed God. O that Christ crucified were the universal burden of men of God.... Blessed is that ministry of which CHRIST IS ALL.

To Charles Haddon Spurgeon the pulpit was the most solemn place in the world. He went to it in manifest dependence on the Holy Spirit. He once said:

We tremble lest we should misbelieve, and tremble more lest we should mistake and misinterpret the Word. I believe Martin Luther would have faced the infernal fiend himself without a fear; and yet we have his own confession that his knees often knocked together when he stood up to preach. He trembled lest he should not be faithful to God's Word. To preach the whole truth is an awful charge. We who are ambassadors for God must not trifle, but we must tremble at God's Word.... A preacher ought to know that he really possesses the Spirit of God, and that when he speaks there is an influence upon him that enables him to speak as God would have him, otherwise out of the pulpit he should go directly; he has no right to be there, he has not been called to preach God's truth.

Spurgeon's preaching was thoroughly Calvinistic. We have seen how the "Doctrines of Grace"—the five points of Calvinism—were expounded at the opening services of the great new Tabernacle. They were consistently preached there by him all the days of his ministry. He was deeply imbued with the ruling principle of Calvin's theology—the Sovereignty of God in creation, providence, and redemption. He wholeheartedly believed that Calvinism was the theology of the Bible, and Evangelicalism as its pure and only stable and adequate expression. He delighted to preach the "five points," but these are not the whole of Calvinism, nor of the truths of Scripture, and Spurgeon pressed home many other facets of the great Genevan's theology, as we shall see in a later chapter.

On April 11, 1861, Spurgeon made a statement about his own doctrinal position in this matter:

The controversy which has been carried on between the Calvinist and the Arminian is exceedingly important, but it does not so involve the vital point of personal godliness as to make eternal life depend on our holding either system of theology.... That doctrine which is called

H.E. [...] Matt XIX. 30. XX. 16.

When saved we begin to serve.

When serving we sh? not forget that we are served.

It will be ill for us if we get into a legal spirit.

I. In the service of our Lord free grace is manifest

  1. All our service is already due.

  2. All our service in itself is unacceptable.

  3. The ability to serve is a gracious gift.

  4. The call is a grace.

  5. The opportunity of the Lord.

  6. The spirit is at to work is wrought in us.

  7. The success is wholly of the Lord.

  8. The honour of suffering a special gift.

II. Hence the Lord has his own way of measuring.

  1. He will reward every worker, but not as we judge.

  2. Not by time, surface covered, labour borne.

  3. Not by ability, mental power, wealth &c

  4. Not by judgment. Others, position in church &c

  5. Not by self-judgment, talk, profession &c

  6. Not by impression made among men.

  7. Not by success.

  8. But by desire, proportion, spirit, thoroughness
      thought of God, love, faith, communion
      By prayer, patient perseverance,
      By that is left, that was not rewarded. &c

Notes for a sermon on "When Saved We Begin to Serve."

"Calvinism" did not spring from Calvin; we believe that it sprang from the great Founder of all truth. Perhaps Calvin derived it mainly from the writings of Augustine. Augustine obtained his views, without doubt, through the Spirit of God, from the diligent study of the writings of Paul, and Paul received them of the Holy Ghost, from Jesus Christ the great Founder of the Christian dispensation.... All the difficulties which are laid against the doctrine of predestination might, with equal force, be laid against that of Divine foreknowledge. God hath predestined all things from the beginning, but there is a difference between the predestination of an intelligent, all-wise, all-bounteous God, and that blind fatalism which simply says, "It is because it is to be." Between the *predestination* of Scripture and the *fate* of the Koran every sensible man must perceive a difference of the most essential character.... I hold God's election, but I testify just as clearly that if any man be lost he is lost for sin.... If he be lost, damnation is all of man; but if he be saved, salvation is all of God....

A charge against us is that we dare not preach the Gospel to the unregenerate, that in fact, our theology is so narrow and cramped that we cannot preach to sinners. Gentlemen, if you dare to say this, I would take you to any library in the world where the old Puritan fathers are stored up, and I would let you take down any one volume and tell me if you ever read more telling exhortations and addresses to sinners in any of your own books. Did not Bunyan plead with sinners, and who ever classed him with any but the Calvinists? Did not Charnock, Goodwin and Howe agonize for souls, and what were they but Calvinists? Did not Jonathan Edwards preach to sinners, and who was more clear and explicit on these doctrinal matters? The works of our innumerable divines teem with passionate appeals to the unconverted.... Did Whitefield's eyes weep the fewer tears or his bowels move with less compassion because he believed in God's electing love and preached the Sovereignty of the Most High? ... I speak of Calvinism proper, as I find it in Calvin's "Institutes," and especially in his Expositions. I have read them carefully. I take not my views of Calvinism from common repute but from his books.... I mean that glorious system which teaches that salvation is of grace from first to last.

Dr. A. C. Underwood, in his *History of the English Baptists,* commits himself to the extraordinary statement that "The truth seems to be that the old Calvinistic phrases were often on Spurgeon's lips, but the genuine Calvinistic meaning had gone out of them."[29] This is manifestly untrue, as anyone who takes the trouble to read the sermons extensively, and who knows what Calvinist doctrines actually are, will soon discover. Further, it makes Spurgeon out to be the utmost hypocrite, using the words but not believing the ideas conveyed by the words. Hypocrite he was not. He used the Calvinist phraseology because he wholeheartedly believed in the Calvinist theology. To him it was nothing less than the theology of the Bible, the revealed truth of the Eternal God. It was the very stuff of his Christian life and outlook, and he sent it forth with every fiber of his being. The idea that Spurgeon, who was a true man of God if ever there was one, should have publicly practiced such deception indicated by Dr. Underwood is thoroughly abhorrent, and quite incredible.

What B. B. Warfield says of John Calvin could, with equal justice, be said of Spurgeon himself:

> As he contemplated the majesty of the Sovereign Father, his whole being bowed in reverence before Him, and his whole heart burned with zeal for His glory. As he remembered that this great God has become in His own Son the Redeemer of sinners, he passionately gave himself to the proclamation of the glory of His grace. Into His hands he committed himself without reserve; his whole spirit wanted to be in all its movements subjected to His government—or, to be more specific, to the "leading of His Spirit." All that was good in him, all the good he hoped might be formed in him, he ascribed to the almighty working of this Divine Spirit. The glory of God alone, and the control of the Spirit, became the twin principles of his whole thought and life.

These principles were Spurgeon's also, wholeheartedly and sincerely so. Yet, as one studies the sermons and compares the later sermons with the earlier ones, one notices that there is a difference. The Calvinism of the earlier sermons is stronger and more aggressive. He hits out more often against the Arminians. The Calvinism of the later sermons, though as decided and downright as ever, is more moderate. The preacher is more mature; he has mellowed; he has given up crude imagery. He has dropped none of his Calvinist theology, but it is sent forth in a sweeter, gentler strain.

---

29. This excerpt is from page 204 of Dr. A. C. Underwood's *History of the English Baptists*.

Dr. Alexander Whyte of Free St. George's, Edinburgh, in one of his lectures on Bunyan's *Grace Abounding* says:

There are times when I cannot enter on my text until I have seen what Mr. Spurgeon has to say upon it. And I felt just in that way about this supreme text tonight. And accordingly I sent up two or three postage stamps to Messrs. Passmore and Alabaster in London and they sent me down by return three sermons by Mr. Spurgeon on this blessed sixth of John. And I read those three sermons with salvation and with thankfulness in my heart, as I always read Spurgeon's sermons, and as multitudes of men and women have read them all the world over. None of us preachers can hold the candle to Spurgeon. I suppose after John Wesley, and perhaps William Booth, Charles Spurgeon will have the most names of saved sinners read out to his everlasting honor on that day when every minister's work shall be revealed. Well, I will give you an example of the way in which that great preacher brings out "the natural force" of this word "him" in this blessed text now open before us—"him that cometh to Me I will in no wise cast out."

"*Him*," says Spurgeon, "means the rich man, the poor man, the great and famous man, and the small and obscure man, the moral man, the man who has been corrupted by sensual pleasures, the man who has sunk into the worst of sins, the man who has climbed to the highest of virtues, he who is next of kin to the devil, and he who is next of kin to the archangel. The sixth of John," continues Spurgeon, "is one of the most gracious and generous texts in the whole Word of God. I cannot tell what kind of men may be in this house tonight; but if burglars are here, and if dynamite men are here, he that comes to Christ this night will in no wise be cast out. If amidst this great congregation there should be some men here whose characters I had better not begin to describe, yet if they come to Christ He will not say one word of rebuke to them, but will welcome them with open arms. Let your past be what it may—wrapped up as it may be in such a mystery of iniquity that nobody would believe it about you; nevertheless, if you come, all your sins will be cast into the depths of the sea. Any 'him' in all the world, let that man come, and it will never be asked where he comes from. If he comes from a slum, or from a spurious tavern, or from a gambling hall, or from a brothel, or from the prison ships—and if he is cast out he will be the first!"

"Powerful as that is," added Dr. Whyte, "it is only one of a thousand illustrations of the way in which Spurgeon in his day pulled so many sinners out of Satan's clutches."

Dr. James Denney, the great Scottish theologian, had a period of what might be called Broad Churchism, says Sir William Robertson Nicoll in the "Appreciation" which introduces the volume of letters Dr. Denney wrote to Sir William.

> [Denney] was reticent in describing his spiritual history, but I believe that his wife, who gave him the truest and most perfect companionship led him into a more pronounced Evangelical creed. It was she who induced him to read Spurgeon, whom he had been inclined to despise. He became an ardent admirer of the preacher and a very careful and sympathetic student of his sermons. It was Spurgeon perhaps as much as anyone who led him to the great decision of his life—the decision to preach the Atoning Death of the Lord Jesus Christ. This, as Dr. Moffatt has said, was all in all to him. He spent and was spent in making it everything to the Church.

It was the evangelical Denney who wrote that masterly book *The Death of Christ.* And it was Charles Haddon Spurgeon who induced him to do it.

We will conclude this study of the Sermons with a passage from one of the early sermons which illustrates how he preached Christ to every class of hearer, and Christ as the only need of every heart:

> Remember, sinner, it is not *your hold* of Christ that saves you—it is Christ; it is not *your joy* in Christ that saves you—it is Christ; it is not even faith in Christ, though that is the instrument—it is Christ's blood and merits; therefore, look not to your hope, but to Christ the source of hope; look not to your faith, but to Christ, the author and finisher of your faith; and if you do that, ten thousand devils cannot throw you down. There is one thing which we all too much confuse in our preaching, namely the great truth that it is *not* prayer, it is *not* faith, it is *not* our doings, it is *not* our feelings upon which we must trust—*but upon Christ, and on Christ alone.* We are apt to think that we are not in a right state, that we do not feel enough, instead of remembering that our business is not with self, but with Christ. Let me beseech you, *look only to Christ*; never expect deliverance from yourself, from ministers, or from any means of any kind apart from Christ; keep your eye simply on Him; let His death, His agonies, His groans, His sufferings, His merits, His glories, His intercession, be fresh upon your mind; when you wake in the morning look to Him; when you lie down at night look for Him.

Truly, he was "the Prince of Preachers."

Chapter 8
His College

I never went to school to Plato or Aristotle....

—JOHN BUNYAN, *GRACE ABOUNDING*

Here is our guide, our rule, ready to direct us in all stated duties, on all occasions and emergencies; so that nothing can befall us, nothing can be required of us in the worship of God, in the course, ways, and actions of our lives, but what we may have here light, guidance, and direction for. It is the word of His wisdom, will, and grace, Who made us these souls, and Who foreknew every thought that would be in them to eternity, and hath secretly laid up in His Word that which shall suit and answer unto every occasion of all that believe in Him.

—JOHN OWEN, *HEBREWS*

There began to grow up around Spurgeon, as his spiritual children, a number of young men who felt an irresistible urge to preach the Gospel. Their lack of education, however, was a real hindrance, and Spurgeon felt that he could not discourage them but do all in his power to equip them for ministry. One of these, T. W. Medhurst, twenty years of age, had been used to the conversion of several people at open-air meetings. Spurgeon, only twenty-one himself, felt that he must help him. So, in July 1855, Medhurst was sent to a Collegiate School at Bexleyheath in Kent, and a year later lived with the Rev. George Rogers, a Congregational minister of Camberwell and a friend of Spurgeon, for guardianship. At first Spurgeon paid the bills, but later the Tabernacle

Church took over the responsibility. In addition, Spurgeon himself taught him theology for two or three hours each week. Medhurst, in due time, was called to a pastorate and did excellent work. Later on, however, he crossed over to America and became head of some strange sect, and appeared arrayed in gorgeous robes, a sad anticlimax for Spurgeon's first student!

Then another young man, E. J. Silverton, applied to Spurgeon for instruction. Spurgeon realized that this also was the call of the Holy Spirit to him, and thus the Pastors' College was commenced. There were eight students, and the Rev. George Rogers was appointed Principal. The College was entirely successful and developed rapidly, and the course lasted two years.

The students were mostly poor and without the educational qualifications that were a prerequisite of other Baptist colleges for their students. Also, and this was a strong point with Spurgeon, he was more than doubtful about the theology taught elsewhere. "It seemed to me," he said, "that the preachers of the grand old truths of the Gospel, ministers suitable for the masses, were more likely to be found in an institution where preaching and divinity would be the main objects, and not degrees and other insignia of human learning." This seems to have relevance today, also, in many quarters. All that Spurgeon insisted on for his students was that they should have been soundly converted, have a definite call from God to preach the Gospel, and have actually preached for two years. The College did not aim to make preachers, but to help those already called. The prospectus for the school said:

> The College aims at training preachers rather than scholars. To develop the faculty of ready speech, to help them to understand the Word of God, and to foster the spirit of consecration, courage, and confidence in God, are objects so important that we put all other matters into a secondary position. If a student should learn a thousand things, and yet fail to preach the Gospel acceptably, his College course will have missed its true design. Should the pursuit of literary prizes and the ambition for classical honors so occupy the mind as to divert his attention from his life work, they are perilous rather than beneficial. To be wise to win souls is the wisdom ministers must possess. [There were no literary prizes!]

> In the Pastors' College, definite doctrines are held and taught. We hold by the doctrines of grace, and the old orthodox faith, and have no sympathy with the countless theological novelties of the present day,

which are novelties only in outward form: in substance they are repetitions of errors exploded long ago. Our standing in doctrinal matters is well known, and we make no profession of latitudinarian charity, yet we find no failure of earnest spirits who rally to our standard, believing that in truth alone can true freedom be found.

The prospectus ended by saying that the President (Spurgeon) had never derived a farthing from the work for himself, and that "at least £100 is required every week to carry on the work." This, of course, was when it had developed and a College building had been erected. At the start it was the day of small things. The students lived at first in the house of the Principal, Mr. Rogers, and then as the numbers grew they were boarded in the neighborhood of the Tabernacle by members of his church, who thought it a great honor to lodge one of Spurgeon's young men.

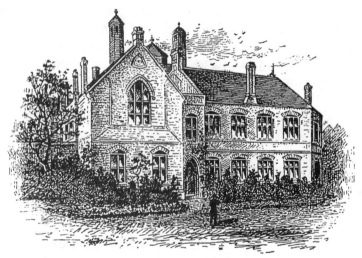

The Pastor's College

Spurgeon was fortunate in the choice of Mr. Rogers as the first Principal, and a deep friendship developed between them. Rogers was an able teacher and deeply versed in theology and other branches of ministerial knowledge. It speaks eloquently for Spurgeon's openness of mind that he trusted his students to the guidance of a paedo-Baptist, but his trust was well rewarded in the spiritual and numerical progress of the College.

The number of students rose steadily. In 1861 there were twenty; in

1862, thirty-nine; in 1863, sixty-six, and within a few more years there were over a hundred. The increase in numbers led to the classes being held in the basement of the Tabernacle, and then land was purchased behind the church and a college block built. Spurgeon laid the foundation stone on October 14, 1873, and the College was opened a year later. It had cost £15,000. Spurgeon himself supplied a good part of the money from the sale of his sermons and books, which produced a regular income additional to his salary, but the Tabernacle Church was also a generous giver. The upkeep of this work was made a special matter of prayer. Sometimes anonymous donors sent large sums; on more than one occasion £1,000 arrived in this way. But there were times of financial strain, and on one occasion the great preacher offered to sell his carriage and horses; but Mr. Rogers and others strenuously opposed this, and somehow the money came in.

Many were the applications received from young men who wished to be trained for the ministry at the Pastors' College. One of them was an engine-driver, who had a little preaching experience. Spurgeon looked at him closely in silence for a while. Suddenly he demanded, "Is the fireman converted?" The engine-driver had to confess that he was not. "Then the footplate is your mission field," said Spurgeon, "come back to me when you have led him to Christ."

One of the greatest influences on the students was Spurgeon's own series of weekly lectures. Every Friday afternoon in term time he would address the men, and this was the event of the week. The two volumes of *Lectures to My Students* are as fresh and as valuable today as when first given, and should be required reading for all theological students and ministers. He lectured on such subjects as "The Minister's Self-Watch," "The Preacher's Private Prayer," "Sermons—their Matter," "The Choice of a Text," "On the Voice," "The Necessity of Ministerial Progress," "Open-Air Preaching," "Posture, Action, Gesture, etc.," this last being illustrated with drawings of odd gesticulations. He had something to say about pulpits also:

> Remarkable are the forms which pulpits have assumed according to the freaks of human fancy and folly. What could have been their design and intent it would be hard to conjecture. A deep wooden pulpit of the old sort might well remind a minister of his mortality, for it is nothing but a coffin set on end: but on what rational ground do we bury our pastors alive? Many of these erections resemble barrels, oth-

ers are of the fashion of egg cups and wine glasses; a third class were evidently modeled after corn bins upon four legs; and yet a fourth variety can only be likened to swallows' nests stuck upon the wall. Some of them are so high as to turn the heads of the occupants when they dare to peer into the awful depths below them, and they give those who look up to the elevated preacher for any length of time a crick in the neck. I have felt like a man at the mast-head while perched aloft in these "towers of the flock".... Frequently, also, a large lamp is placed close to each side of the minister's head, thus cramping all his movements, and placing him between two fires. If any complaints are made of the hotheadedness of our ministers, it is readily to be accounted for, since the apparatus for the purpose is arranged with great care. No one in erecting a pulpit seems to think of the preacher as a man of like feelings and senses with other people; the seat upon which you are to rest at intervals is often a mere ledge, and the door handle runs into the small of your back....

He gave also lectures on "The Puritans," on Christian classics like the *Confessions of St. Augustine*, the *Imitation of Christ*, etc., and The *Holy Spirit in our Ministry.* Sometimes there would be readings, and comments, from the poets—Milton, Young, Cowper, Wordsworth and Coleridge; and how beautifully he read them! He also gave a series of lectures on commentaries, and his volume *Commenting and Commentaries* is one of the most useful books he compiled.

Many sneers were expressed then, and since, concerning Spurgeon's lack of scholarship. Certainly by university standards he could not be termed a scholar, perhaps, nor did he ever claim to be such. But he was far more learned and well read than his detractors realized. Dr. W. Wright of the Bible Society, and his neighbor at Upper Norwood, tells how he came upon Spurgeon in his study one day, with a Greek lexicon on one side of him, and a Hebrew lexicon on the other. Dr. Fullerton who knew him well, said that he had "a great weight of learning, but it was never his habit to parade it."

In 1932 in a series of articles in *The Times*, Dr. Reaveley Glover of St. John's College, Cambridge, Public Orator of the University and President of the Baptist Union, made a strong attack on Spurgeon. He said that he had "an untrained mind, without the discipline of ordered study," and that he "prepared young men for the Baptist ministry in a rather amateur way," and that less famous men "possessed a wider intellectual range and outlook." The bad taste of this outpouring was answered in *The Times* by the Rev. Tydeman Chilvers, one of Spurgeon's successors at the Metropolitan Tabernacle.

The students were given opportunities to preach in churches, mission halls, and in the open air, in order to develop their gifts. There was also a weekly sermon class, in which the students had to preach before students and staff and often got short shrift from Spurgeon, but as often warm encouragement. They had also the incomparable privilege of hearing Spurgeon on Sundays and Thursdays at the Metropolitan Tabernacle—a ministerial education in itself. He helped and guided many of them to their ultimate spheres of ministry, sending some to almost dead churches to revive them, and others to initiate churches in places where there was a need, he himself often paying for the hire of a hall for a year in which a student might preach and gather a congregation. He it was who sent Dr. F. W. Boreham, the prolific author, to his life work in Australasia.[30]

The Rev. D. J. Hiley, one of his students, feelingly described his first meeting with "the Guv'nor," as Spurgeon was affectionately called by his students:

> I can never discharge my debt to C. H. Spurgeon. In him I saw the very face of God. I knew him intimately from 1884 to the day of his death in 1892. Those years were among the keenest years of my life, and the impression of that period will never be effaced. As a young, married man, who had undertaken the pastorate of a small church in the Forest of Dean, I only had about half a dozen sermons, and I very soon got to the end of them. I deeply felt the need of further equipment for the Christian ministry, and applied to Spurgeon. On July 30, 1884, I received a letter from Mr. Spurgeon, saying that the fact that I was married was a real difficulty, rents in London were high, and it was scarcely possible for me to live as a student and support a wife and family. So far the letter was very discouraging. But it ended with an offer of thirty shillings a week, if I cared to come into the College at the beginning of the next term.
>
> "Is that your best coat?" Spurgeon asked me one day when we met in a corridor. "Yes, Sir," I answered. Spurgeon pondered a moment, and then made a suggestion. "I wonder if you would render me a little service?" I replied, "I'd walk my feet off for you." But Spurgeon said, "I don't want you to do that. You'll want your feet later on." The service

---

30. Australia, New Zealand, and neighboring islands in the South Pacific Ocean.

he required was the delivery of a letter at a certain tailor's shop. I was to wait for a reply. The next thing I knew, the tailor measured me for a new suit of clothes and an overcoat, and sent me away with a hat-box! This incident is an illustration of what always impressed me—Spurgeon's wonderful humanness, and great tenderness.

Spurgeon established a fine college library, richly endowed, of course, with Puritan authors. He inaugurated an annual College Conference, held in the spring, attended by Pastors' College trained ministers, and always addressed by himself and other notable preachers of all denominations.

By the time of his death nearly 900 men had been trained for the Baptist ministry at his college, or who proceeded to various mission fields, and many of them became eminent in the work of the Lord—like Dr. F. W. Boreham. The College has also had some outstanding scholars and Christian leaders as Principals during its history. It would hardly be too much to say that the Pastors' College revitalized the Baptist denomination. The impact of 900 men in his lifetime, grounded in Puritan theology and the fundamental truths of Holy Scripture, was great indeed.

Some years after Spurgeon's death, the College—now named "Spurgeon's College"—was transferred to South Norwood, where it still trains men for the ministry, and where Spurgeon's name and fame is held in reverence.

The Stockwell Orphanage

Chapter 9
His Orphanage

Is it nothing for a man to be employed in comforting, relieving, and supporting others? This is so great a service that the very angels are employed therein, as in the work most suitable to them.... How many poor, drooping, tempted, and deserted souls are there whom you may go and minister to.

—WILLIAM BRIDGE, *A LIFTING UP FOR THE DOWNCAST*

Prayer was one open secret of the success and blessing of the Metropolitan Tabernacle, and mighty were their weekly prayer meetings. The atmosphere was often deeply charged with the power of the Holy Spirit. But Spurgeon believed that faith and prayer should issue in good works. At one prayer meeting he said, "We are a large church, and should be doing more for the Lord in this great city. I want us to ask Him to send us some new work; and if we need money to carry it on, let us pray that the money may also be sent." The Lord lost no time in setting a new challenge before them.

One day not long afterwards, Spurgeon received a letter from a Mrs. Hillyard, widow of a clergyman. She belonged to the "Brethren," was rich, and determined to devote her money to the service of God. She decided to place it in Spurgeon's hands. She had read an article in Spurgeon's magazine, *The Sword and the Trowel* for August 1866, which urged the establishment of schools for the children of poor believers. It was laid on her heart that an orphanage would be pleasing to God.

Spurgeon regarded this as a direct answer to prayer. Mrs. Hillyard had no less a sum than £20,000 for the purpose, and before long with his deacon and builder friend, William Higgs, Spurgeon called on her to discuss the matter. Very concerned that the will of God be done he first asked whether there was not some relative of hers who should receive the money. There was not. Should she not, Spurgeon then suggested, send the money to George Müller of Bristol, who was very experienced with regard to orphans and orphanages? No, she insisted, Spurgeon himself must have it and inaugurate the work. And so the munificent gift was accepted, and the orphanage established.

The boys' side of the orphanage

It was most necessary, Spurgeon thought, that the orphanage should be in easy reach of the Tabernacle, so that the children could be brought under the sound of the Gospel. A suitable and extensive site was found in Clapham Road, Stockwell. The project raised widespread interest and money poured in. Several individuals or groups paid the whole cost of some of the houses. The foundation stone was laid on August 9, 1867, and the boys' section was completed, free of debt, in 1869. The houses for the orphans were neatly ranged round a wide greensward, and in addition there was a hall for assembly purposes, dining hall, gymnasium, main infirmary, and offices. The girls' section came into being in the years 1879-1880. The Rev. Vernon S. Charlesworth was appointed headmaster, and a staff of convinced Christians enlisted.

The Stockwell Orphanage was ever dear to Spurgeon's heart; he loved children, and he always received an uproarious welcome when he appeared there. And he was constantly there. Children from all denominations were received, and no distinctive dress was worn. It was an impressive sight to see 500 children, 250 boys and 250 girls, assembled each Sunday in front of the pulpit at the Tabernacle, listening to their benefactor.

The God that answers by orphanages, let Him be God!" declared Spurgeon, in answer to an agnostic professor who denied the being of God. It was a sound reply.

The girls' side of the orphanage

Friends of the Orphanage continually sent gifts for the work. One sent £10,000, and another sent thousands of shirts for the boys. Others sent food, shoes, socks, dresses. One day Mr. Charlesworth was given six-dozen bunches of turnips by a greengrocer. "You may have them for the orphans if you like," he said, "and I hope somebody else will send the mutton." Somebody else did. An hour or two later a whole sheep, fattened and killed especially for the Orphanage, was delivered by a farmer. That all the wants of the children should be supplied was Spurgeon's unshakable conviction. "If we get to the bottom of the barrel of meal," he once remarked, "the Lord will hear the scraping and then He will fill it up again!"

At a meeting of the Trustees on one occasion, Spurgeon reported, "Well, we're cleared out; we must go to the great Chancellor of the Exchequer," and the matter was laid before God in prayer. The following Sunday morning he reported to the deacons that £850 had come in. Again in 1874 when funds were nearly exhausted and the flow of income had subsided almost to a trickle, the need of the orphans was again made a matter of special prayer. Not long afterwards Spurgeon was handed a gift of £10,000 for his work, half of which was for the Orphanage. Year by year gifts, legacies, and church offerings continued to provide for all the needs, and came from all parts of Britain and Europe.

One wise arrangement at the Orphanage was the separate house system; each house being a distinct family in itself, with a real "mother," to whom each child could look up. Thus a family spirit, rather than an institutional one, prevailed. Family worship was conducted in each house. The education provided was of a high standard.

Mr. Spurgeon with the boys at the orphanage

To the large-hearted Spurgeon the Stockwell Orphanage was ever dear. Much of his time was devoted to its concerns and the well-being of the boys and girls. Once a week he breakfasted with the Trustees in order to discuss business. He was a frequent visitor, often taking distinguished persons such as Lord Shaftesbury over the buildings. For many years he spent each Christmas Day with the children, happy and lively times indeed.

The author well remembers as a child, attending with his parents for many years, the annual Founder's Day Festival at the Stockwell Orphanage. These were great occasions indeed. There was the interest of looking over the houses, and strolling on the lawns, and having tea in a marquee; and, to crown all, the great evening meeting when the

Assembly Hall was crowded, and the children's choir sang sacred and secular items, some of the children recited, and—most splendid of all—a team of child hand-bell ringers performed with great ability. It was perfectly obvious that the Orphanage was a very happy place, made blessed with the love of God and of man.

The Orphanage is renamed "Spurgeon's Homes" and functions in a splendid group of houses set amidst spacious and beautiful grounds at Birchington in Kent, by the seaside. Here 200 boys and girls are lovingly cared for in the spirit of the founder.

Thousands of boys and girls have passed through the Homes, coming from all denominational backgrounds. They have entered a great variety of vocations and professions, while several have been called to the ministry or gone forth to the mission field. A number have become company directors, partners in old-established firms, or captains of industry. One, John Morgan, sat in the House of Commons as MP for Doncaster; another, Stephen Warrington, became a popular BBC broadcaster; while yet another, David Kingdon, became Principal of the Irish Baptist College, Belfast. It is interesting to note that the secretaries have all been old boys of the Home. The 1934 Festival, during the Spurgeon Centenary celebrations, was honored by the smiling presence of H.R.H.[31] the Duchess of York, now Queen Elizabeth the Queen Mother.

While no pressure is ever put on the boys and girls to make a profession of faith, it is always the prayer of those who care for them that every one of them will, before leaving, come to know Christ as a living reality and personal Savior.

This may be the place to mention other philanthropic works helped on or inaugurated by Spurgeon. When the New Park Street Chapel was sold, the money was devoted to rebuilding the Almshouses connected with the Church, which had been established by his predecessor Dr. Rippon. Here many of the old and homeless found a refuge and a friend.

The number and variety of the auxiliary organizations of the Metropolitan Tabernacle, and the amount of energy Spurgeon put into them, is amazing. There were forty-nine mission Bible schools; there was the Christian Brothers Benefit Society, The Evangelists' Association and

---

31. This abbreviation refers to "His (or Her) Royal Highness."

Country Mission, The Flower Mission, The Gospel Temperance Society, The Ladies' Benevolent Society, The Ladies' Maternal Society, The Tract Society, The Poor Ministers' Clothing Society, The Ragged Schools, The Pioneer Mission, The Lay Preachers, and a few more! If he did not run them all he was closely concerned with their affairs, and gave freely of his time and money to them. In many cases he acted as treasurer of these societies, and bemoaned the Haddon in his name—he was named after a benefactor friend of his father—when it came to writing hundreds of checks. Susannah said, and who should know better than she: "There never was a busier life than his; not an atom more of sacred service could have been crowded into it."

And the Colportage[32] Association must not be forgotten. This was founded in September 1866, with its headquarters in the College building. Spurgeon, who was a country lad and remembered his own rural days, was concerned that people in country places, out of touch with Evangelical churches, and out of reach of bookshops, and who for the most part were poor, should have an opportunity to secure copies of the Scriptures, and good Evangelical books at low cost. This, too, came to pass by the good hand of God. He organized it in a statesmanlike way, dividing up the country into areas, and suggesting the books to be secured. At one time there were ninety-six peddlers of books in various regions, selling books from door to door, and in country marketplaces. In one year 23,000 Bibles were sold. Not only did the workers sell books, but they spoke to the country folk on their doorsteps about the salvation of their souls, pointed men and women to Christ, prayed with the sick and dying, and held open-air meetings. This was a work very dear to the heart of Spurgeon, and constantly prayed for at the Tabernacle. It is a sign of the growing apostasy of our times that most door-to-door work is now carried on by the followers of false cults whose literature only deceives the unwary and promotes error.

One last characteristic word. Spurgeon said in the course of a sermon on the love of Christ, "I pray God, that this church, whether it carries on its orphan houses, or its College, or its Colportage, or whatever else it does, may do it all for Jesus."

It was all done for Jesus!

---

32. This term refers to the distribution of Bibles, religious tracts, and books; this work was done by a *colporteur*—a peddler of books.

Chapter 10
Heir of the Puritans

Christ's offering Himself was the greatest expression of His inexpressible love. To fancy that there is any cleansing from sin but by the blood of Christ, is to overthrow the Gospel. We are never nearer Christ than when we find ourselves lost in a holy amazement at His unspeakable love.

—JOHN OWEN, *THE GLORY OF CHRIST*

Charles Haddon Spurgeon was completely molded and fashioned by those spiritual giants of the sixteenth and seventeenth centuries, the Puritans. He stood in their noble tradition, in the direct line of their theology and outlook, and can without question be called *the heir of the Puritans.*

THE PURITANS

It may be well to refresh our minds concerning these great men of old. The Puritans were a body of men of God who brought a spiritual light to England, and stamped a moral greatness upon her that no other group, religious or secular, has ever done. Yet no people have been more persistently maligned and misrepresented than they. The very word Puritan has become in many quarters a term of scorn, implying a gloomy fanaticism, hypocrisy, narrow-minded and illiterate bigotry, and so on. Today, if anyone stands up for clear-cut biblical doctrines and simple worship, or sets himself against moral declension, political unrighteousness, apostasy in the church, gambling, drinking and unwholesome amusements, or the secularization of the Lord's Day, he is sure to be derided as "puritanical." The hatred of the Puritans was deliberately fostered by their political and ecclesiastical enemies in the reign of Charles the Second, many of whom were the avowed enemies of truth and godliness. But the term Puritan is really a badge of honor; part of the reproach of Christ, borne by men not afraid or ashamed to gather to Him "without the camp."

The Puritan movement extended from about 1560, when Elizabeth I was enforcing conformity in liturgy and ceremonial, until 1688, the year of the Glorious Revolution, when William of Orange, "the royal Calvinist," banished the Stuarts from the throne. But the Puritans were only in the ascendancy and control of the government for about twenty years, 1640-1660, under the Lord Protector, Oliver Cromwell.

Puritanism began as a reform movement in the Church of England against all tendencies toward the Church of Rome. In 1572 the Puritans drew up a statement of their position called "The Admonition" which they presented to the government. They protested that many ministers had no true call from God and were ignorant and inefficient; they urged that only those things which God's Word commanded should be placed in churches or expressed in worship; they objected to the use of the surplice[33] because they regarded it as a priestly garment, to the sign of the cross in baptism as superstitious, to kneeling at the Lord's Supper as implying adoration of the elements of bread and wine; and to the observance of sundry festivals as of pagan origin. They desired to purge from the services all remnants of Roman Catholic teaching, practice, and superstition, and to procure in every parish an earnest, spiritually-minded, preaching minister. Their principles were rejected.

At the accession of James the First in 1603 there were more than one-thousand Puritan clergy, strong in Reformed theology and Reformed practices. Side by side with this movement in the Church of England grew the Separatist movement—Independents, Presbyterians, Baptists, etc., later to become the Free Churches of the land. Their principles largely coalesced. Later with the Act of Uniformity of 1662 and the ejection of the Puritans from the State Church, the name Puritan was usually applied to Nonconformists.

Three vital factors largely contributed to the growth and progress of

---

33. A loose, white, wide-sleeved outer vestment worn by the clergy in the Church of England.

Puritanism: the founding of Emmanuel College, Cambridge, the Puritan College, where scores of the finest Evangelical divines were trained (we have already noted this seat of Puritan piety in a previous chapter); the production of the "Westminster Confession of Faith," which with the Longer and Shorter Catechism and the Directory of Public Worship was drawn up by the Westminster Assembly of Divines in 1647, and sets forth the Puritan system of faith and gives a comprehensive definition of Calvinist doctrine with Scriptural proofs; and the voluminous writings both doctrinal and practical of Puritan authors. After 1662, when many of their voices were silenced, their pens were busier than ever. Richard Baxter alone wrote no less than 168 books. The great Puritan names, as we have seen, are Goodwin, Baxter, Owen, Brooks, Charnock, Manton, Sibbes, Howe, Marshall, Watson, Ness, Poole-Conner, Bunyan, Bridges, Calamy, Flavel, Bifield, and many more.

The great foundation principles of the Puritans ought to be remembered. The Puritans carried to its logical conclusion the great Protestant Reformation emphasis on the Bible as the only rule of faith and conduct. To the Puritans, the Bible was the very Voice and Message of God to men; it was the infallible and authoritative work of the Holy Spirit. They maintained that it was primary and fundamental for determining doctrine, worship, and church government. The Spirit in the Scriptures spoke to the Puritan not only of man's sin and salvation provided freely by Christ, and of the ordering of His church and worship, but also concerning the civil and political problems of the day, even concerning daily toil, home life, dress, recreation, and duty. They surveyed the whole gamut of life in the light of God's Word, and His revealed truth was implicitly trusted and obeyed.

Further, the Puritan was deeply concerned to worship God in the beauty of holiness. He was distrustful of much art and music in worship, although he valued both in their proper place. Cromwell delighted in music; music and dancing has a place in *Pilgrim's Progress*. It was their deep conviction that there must be simplicity, purity, and reality in worship, and that the trappings of ceremonial and outward adornment would hinder men from hearing the voice of God. This it was that made the Puritans so determined to purge worship of Roman accretions, and restore biblical simplicity and purity. The central place of the pulpit in the Church, with the communion table below it, was deliberate. It was to exalt not the preacher but the Word of God. The

Bible, prominently enthroned on its pulpit cushion, was witness to its authority in the church. The Puritans developed congregational singing in place of the service being sung by the choir or clergy. Nothing so angered the Puritans as unworthy clergy trafficking in unholy things or adulterating the oracles of God. They stood for a converted, Scriptural, prayerful, educated, and energetic ministry, such a ministry, indeed, as Baxter's, great book *The Reformed Pastor* extols. In the Puritan view the grace of God was mediated to men through a consecrated personality preaching the Word of God, rather than through the sacraments or the ritual of worship. Elaborate buildings, decorations, ceremonial vestments, and music were regarded as superfluous, unedifying, and distracting. Simplicity and purity on the Bible pattern was their aim.

Richard Baxter

Puritan preaching was Scriptural, evangelical, doctrinal, experimental, practical, and comprehensive. They preached long sermons, generally an hour or more, and they divided and subdivided their matter so that it was easy to follow and take in, and to be remembered. Sometimes they reached "twentiethly," and each division might have six or ten subdivisions. The habit of many divisions arose from their training in logic at the universities. But such was the love of the Puritans for God's Word that they eagerly sought to explore a subject in an exhaustive and thoroughgoing way, and to leave no possible shade of meaning or application unconsidered. The impact of this method on Spurgeon's sermons is easy to see at a glance. They were his masters, and he drank deep of their ways as well as of their spirit.

The aim of the Puritan preaching and writing was not merely to interest and uplift, but to make a man face himself in the light of a holy, pardoning God, ponder the path of his feet, wrestle with his conscience, and apply God's truth and grace to his own condition. The Puritans sent their arrows to the mark; they went into details, and particularized sins and temptations and trials and conditions of soul. They said, like the prophet, "Thou art the man!" They analyzed and probed and searched, and let the searchlight of God's Word and the pruning-knife of the Holy Spirit expose and cleanse the inmost depths of their listeners. No wonder the ungodly and libertines and Cavaliers could not stand it. It left them no refuge but Christ. Puritan preaching made men tremble before the Throne of Holiness, and drove them to the Mercy-seat. It was Christ-centered from first to last, and drew or drove men to the Savior.

In our day the Puritan writings are being reprinted and studied widely. An annual "Puritan and Reformed Studies Conference"[34] is held at Westminster Chapel, which is bringing many ministers, especially younger ones, into the old paths of truth. The effect of this on the future of the Church will surely be great indeed.

Under the Puritans, also, family worship and Bible reading became national customs, and continued long after the Puritan era. Indeed, these grand aids to personal religion were introduced by the Puritans.

One other dominating principle must be considered. The Puritans emphasized the sovereignty of God, and the need for absolute obedience to His will. They had a keen sense of their responsibility to God both for themselves and for other men. They lived their lives with deep seriousness as in the sight of Almighty God, and in the presence of Eternity. Puritanism was the creed of men in deadly earnest about the worth of the soul, the judgment of God, and the duty of pleasing the Lord. It was from these considerations that there sprang their convic-

---

34. This conference was originally founded by Dr. Martin Lloyd-Jones.

tions of human rights and civil liberties. The supreme principle of Calvinism, the sovereignty of God in creation, providence, and redemption, gripped them and regulated their lives and their theology. They desired and strove that God should be king in their personal lives, Parliament and affairs of State, the army, the church, and the life of the nation. The Puritan opposition to the theater and drama of their time had every justification, chiefly because, as in ancient Rome, it had become debased in the service of lust, as anyone can judge for himself who reads the plays of the period, especially the Restoration comedies. The Puritans were not alone in their condemnation of the theater, so were the London aldermen, several of the bishops, and sundry Jesuits. The diarists John Evelyn (a royalist) and Samuel Pepys (a naval official) often record their disgust at the plays they saw, and condemned the degeneration and licentiousness of the stage. As to recreation, the Puritans opposed bear-baiting, cock-fighting, rope-walking, dancing, May Day revels, etc., because too often they were associated with drunkenness, gambling, brutality, and impurity. Today, when so many of our amusements are debased and debasing, a Puritan censorship of the theater, cinema, television, and literature would provide a healthy cleansing of our national life.

The Puritan conception of life "under the Great Taskmaster's eye," as John Milton, the Puritan poet, expresses it, or under the hand of God, meant seriousness, watchfulness, discipline, high regard for duty in every walk of life. It is a matter of historical fact that the practical outworking of the Puritan ethic in trade and industry often led to great prosperity and wealth. If this came, then God has sent it, they firmly believed. The Puritan looked on his talents and possessions as a stewardship for which he was responsible to give account to God. We surely have much to learn from them in matters like these. Much that is best in our moral life today, and in our civil and religious liberties, we derive from the maligned Puritans.

One of the greatest of the Puritans, Richard Sibbes, of St. John's College, Cambridge, preacher of Gray's Inn, London, says this of preaching:

> The special work of our ministry is to lay open Christ, to hold up the tapestry and unfold the mysteries of Christ. Let us labor therefore to be always speaking somewhat about Christ, or tending that way. When we speak of the law, let it drive us to Christ; when of moral duties, let

them teach us to walk worthy of Christ. Christ, or something tending to Christ, should be our theme and mark to aim at.

That is the heart and crown of Puritanism. They were always "tending to Christ." God raised them up not only for a light to their own age, but for all time. It is our privilege and responsibility as heirs of the Puritans to strive together for the truth of God, the simplicity of the Gospel, the purity of the Church, and the faith given to the saints, as they did; relying always, as they did, on the Spirit and Power of the Lord, and submitting everything to His divine sovereignty.

PURITAN THEOLOGY

Charles Haddon Spurgeon was steeped in these principles, outlook, and writings. From his earliest days in his grandfather's parsonage at Stambourne, he had begun to read the Puritans. They were his favorite authors. None could be compared with them for doctrinal soundness, strengthening of faith, sweetness of comfort, and heart-searching and Christ-exalting thought. All his life he lit his torch from their fire, and in his hand it burned brightly throughout his entire ministry. Heir of the Puritans indeed!

He was a great reader and collector of Puritan works and at his death there were 12,000 volumes in his library, among which 7,000 were Puritan books. He searched catalogs for them, ransacked bookstalls, and poked about in shops. He hunted originals, not reprints. "I harbor a prejudice against all new editions," he said, "and a preference for the originals even though they wander about in sheepskins and goatskins, and are shut up in the heaviest of board."

And he read them and got Susannah to read them. He delved into them as one that finds great spoil. He stored their deep truths and pithy sayings in his mind so as to quote them in his sermons with ease or to locate the source in the book he might require. In his Mentone retirements[35] as well as on his holidays he always carried a Puritan book on his walks in order to dip into it when he took a rest. Their emphasis and outlook became his at all points.

Which were the Puritan books he loved most? The following were

---

35. These *retirements* refer to the times Spurgeon and his wife withdrew into the seclusion of Menton, France (*Mentone* in Italian). This winter-resort city is located in southeastern France along the Mediterranean Sea.

Richard Sibbes

read over and over again by him: *Apples of Gold* by Thomas Brooks, and also his *Precious Remedies Against Satan's Devices*, but he delighted in all the books of this writer; *The Objects and Acts of Justifying Faith* by Goodwin; Owen on *The Glories of Christ, The Death of Death in the Death of Christ, The Holy Spirit,* and *Hebrews*; *The Attributes of God,* a massive work by Charnock; *The Christian in Complete Armour* by Gurnall; *John 17* by Manton; *Mystery of Providence* by Flavel; *The Body of Divinity* by Thomas Watson he highly valued, and reissued it with a biographical introduction and an Appendix on Believers' Baptism, for the use of his students; Baxter's *Reformed Pastor* and *Saints' Everlasting Rest*; and, of course, Bunyan's *Pilgrim's Progress* and *The Holy War.*

It must not, however, be thought that his was a narrow or a one-track mind; he was a man of wide reading. Literature, biography, travel, science, history, poetry, as well as theology interested him. He read all Shakespeare's plays, some of them many times. Boswell's *Life of Johnson* was a favorite which he read again and again. He was not unacquainted with Scott, Dickens, and Trollope, though he much disliked the anti-Evangelical bias of the two latter. His library covered all the most important subjects that have interested the human mind, and he often sent his secretary, Mr. Harrald, to the British Museum library to garner extra information. He read rapidly, making it a point to read half a dozen of the meatiest books per week. He would sit down to five or six large books and master their contents at a sitting. W. T. Stead, the famous journalist, set him a friendly test of his grip of four or five books read one afternoon, and he came through it with amazing ability, to Stead's admiration.

His chief Book, however, was the Bible. "It is blessed to eat into the very soul of the Bible," he said, "until at last you come to talk in Scriptural language, and your spirit is flavored with the words of the Lord, so that your blood is *Bibline*,[36] and the very essence of the Bible flows from you. Hundreds of times have I surely felt that presence of God in the page of Scripture."

The Bible and the Puritans formed his theology, and he did not depart from it one hairsbreadth all his life. Never for one moment did he waver in his conviction that the truth he had learned as a boy was everything. "Narrow-minded," "bigoted," "crude," "ignorant," "obscurantist" were some of the terms of reproach heaped upon him, but he cared not one whit for such criticisms. He was unshakably sure that he had the root and the substance of the matter, and if others differed from him on the supreme points of truth, be they prince or prelate or college professor, so much the worse for them!

Someone, some day, will write a book about the theology of Spurgeon, and a rich volume it will be—always providing that the author is in sympathy with Spurgeon's views. To see him as the heir of the Puritans it will be well for us briefly to examine some of the vital and fundamental doctrines which he held dear, and which he preached from first to last.

1. *The Divine Inspiration and Authority of Scripture*

He believed the entire Bible to be the Word of God, and rested his whole faith on it. To Spurgeon it was the divine revelation of eternal truth, God-breathed in every part, and therefore absolutely inerrant, infallible, and wholly trustworthy and reliable for faith and conduct. In

---

36. The suffix *-ine* means *of* or *having the nature of* some thing or some one; therefore, this term carries the connotation of being filled and completely absorbed with the Bible.

1888 he reissued for the use of his students *Theopneustia: the Plenary Inspiration of the Holy Scriptures,* by Dr. L. Gaussen, Professor of Systematic Theology at Geneva. In the preface that he wrote for this spiritual classic, Spurgeon said:

> The turning-point in the battle between those who hold the "faith once delivered to the saints'"and their opponents lies in the true and real inspiration of the Holy Scriptures. This is the Thermopylae[37] of Christendom. If we have in the Word of God no infallible standard of truth, we are at sea without a compass. "If the foundations be removed, what can the righteous do?" and this is a foundation loss of the worst kind.... We can have a measure of fellowship with a mistaken friend who is willing to bow before the teaching of Scripture if he can be made to understand it; but we must part company altogether with the one who believes in error—who overrides prophets and apostles, and practically regards his own inspiration as superior to theirs. We fear that such a man will before long prove himself to be an enemy of the cross of Christ, all the more dangerous because he will profess loyalty to the Lord Whom he dishonors. It is a delight to turn from the fantasies of the new school to the certainties of the Word of God.

2. *The Sovereignty of God*

Spurgeon ever loved to magnify and exalt the Lord in His supreme and sovereign rule over all men and all events. He is sovereign in creation, providence, and grace. Spurgeon firmly held that God was Architect, Maker, Sustainer, Provider and Controller of the entire universe, and man in it. That His will was almighty and everlasting and unchangeable and perfectly right and good. In His wisdom and love He upholds and rules all things, and we can only say, "Even so, Father, for so it seemed good in Thy sight." It is ours not to question or rebel, but to trust and obey. He preached to debase man and to enthrone the Lord, but then he firmly believed in the depravity of man and the holiness of God, the inability of man to do good apart from divine grace, and the unutterable, yet merciful, majesty of God. Yet, divine sovereignty did not annul human responsibility; man was answerable to

---

37. A mountain pass in the Locris region of ancient Greece (north of the Gulf of Corinth), near an inlet of the Aegean Sea; here a famous battle took place in which the Persians under Xerxes destroyed the Spartan army under Leonidas in 480 BC.

God and must respond to Him. But man could not finally resist God, still less could he "help" God, as the modern notion has it.

Stephen Charnock

3. Predestination and Election

He loved the great Calvinist doctrines of sovereign grace in God's choice and redemption of His people, and did not shrink from pressing them upon his hearers. But he handled these deep Scriptural themes gently and in a balanced proportion with respect to other truths. God's people were elected by God the Father, redeemed by God the Son, and sanctified by God the Holy Spirit. Salvation was all of God, in the Trinity of His Persons, from first to last.

"He will have mercy on whom He will have mercy." He saves because He will save. And if you ask me why He saves me, I can only say, because He would do it. Was there anything in me that should recommend me to God? No, I lay aside everything. I have nothing to recommend me. When God saved me I was the most abject, lost and ruined of the race. I lay before Him as an infant in my blood. I had no power to help myself. Oh, how wretched did I feel and know myself to be....

But God from the beginning chose His people; when the unnavigated atmosphere was yet unfanned by the wing of a single angel, when space was shoreless or yet unborn, when universal silence reigned, when there was no being, and no motion, no time, and naught but God Himself, alone in His eternity ... in the beginning He chose them unto eternal life.

"Ah, but," say some, "I thought it meant that God elected some to heaven and some to hell." That is a very different matter from the Gospel doctrine. He has elected men to holiness and to righteousness, and through that to heaven. He has elected you to holiness, if you love holiness. If any of you love to be saved by Jesus Christ, He elected you to be saved. If any of you desire to have salvation, you are elected to have it, if you desire it sincerely and earnestly. But if you do not desire it, why on earth should you be so preposterously foolish as to grumble because God gives that which you do not like to other people?

> Sons we are through God's election,
> Who by Jesus Christ believe;
> By eternal destination
> Sovereign grace is here received.

If you believe on the Lord Jesus Christ you are elect.

4.   The Deity of Christ

The eternal Godhead and excellence of the Son of God was a constant theme. To Spurgeon, the Lord Jesus Christ, the "Well-beloved" as he used to call Him, was the Son of God, coequal and coeternal with the Father, possessed of omniscience and supernatural power. He was a strong opponent of all Unitarians[38] and Socinians.[39] He strenuously

---

38. A religious sect founded on the doctrine that God is one being, rejecting the biblical doctrine of the Trinity; this group emphasizes tolerance of difference in religious opinions, thus denying the uniqueness of Christian truth.

39. Followers of Faustus and Laelius Socinus who rejected the Trinity, the Divinity of Christ, and original sin; this nephew-uncle duo was from Italy and lived during the time of the Protestant Reformation.

affirmed our Lord's virgin, supernatural birth, His sinless life, His unique knowledge of God and His will and truth, and of the human heart and events. It was His being very God that gave unique worth to His sacrificial death upon the Cross and made it a divine act of atonement for sinners. If He were not the Son of God and the Redeemer of men, then He was a liar and deceiver.

> As a King, He is described as sitting upon His own throne. He has not usurped the throne of another, but His right to sovereignty is indisputable. He has well deserved to be King of men since He is their Redeemer. His Father has given Him a crown as the reward of His travail. He sits upon a throne which He has won by conquest, for He has vanquished the powers of darkness and led captivity captive. There is no Monarch so secure as He. He is really and truly King by right divine. He is King by descent, for He is Son and heir of the Highest. He is King by His own intrinsic excellence, for there is none to be compared to Him. And He is King by His own native might and majesty, for He Himself holds the throne against all comers, and shall hold it till all enemies shall be under His feet.

5. The Substitutionary Atonement of Christ

This was an exceedingly precious doctrine to Spurgeon, and one strenuously opposed by "modernists" then and now. He affirmed with all his strength and eloquence that, for our redemption, Christ became the sinner's Substitute and Sin-bearer. Christ died in the sinner's place and stead, the Just for the unjust, the spotless One for the guilty one, laying down His life as the Good Shepherd for and on behalf of His sheep. He was convinced that there was no other meaning in Scripture to the death of Christ. That death was no mere martyrdom, nor example of love and fortitude, but a transaction with God on behalf of ruined, lost, and guilty sinners, who were quite incapable of saving themselves. His blood was shed as a ransom for many. His death paid the price to set men free. He bore the wrath of God on account of sin for His chosen, that they might never bear it. His death was a substitutionary sacrifice. "By His stripes we are healed."

> The doctrine of the atonement is very simple. It just consists in the substitution of Christ in the place of the sinner; Christ being treated as if He were the sinner, and then the transgressor being treated as if he were the righteous one. It is a change of persons; Christ becomes the sinner; He stands in the sinner's place and stead, and is numbered

with the transgressors; the sinner becomes righteous, and he stands in Christ's place and stead, and is numbered with the righteous ones. Christ has no sin of His own, but He takes human guilt, and is punished for human folly. We have no righteousness of our own, but we take the divine righteousness; we are rewarded for it, and stand accepted before God as though that righteousness had been wrought out by ourselves.

Spurgeon gloried in the Cross and in the sacrifice of Christ as a Substitute for guilty men. Like Paul he loved to declare, "God commendeth His love towards us, in that, while we were yet sinners, Christ died for us" (Romans 5:8). Once the Rev. Robert Taylor, Presbyterian minister of Upper Norwood, called on him and asked if he could put into a few words his Christian faith. "It is all in four words," he replied, "Jesus died for me!"

6. *Justification by Faith alone*

Luther's article of a standing or a falling church was a great theme of Spurgeon, as it was of the Reformers, the Puritans, and the men of the Evangelical Revival. Dearly did he love to proclaim that "God is Just, and the Justifier of him who believes in Jesus." Justice has been satisfied through the substitution of the Son of God for us, and through the Second Adam God is able to forgive the vilest of the vile, and acquit, accept, and take as His child, all who believe on His Son.

> Faith looks back upon the pardoned past, and rests herself upon the faithfulness and power of God to save. At times these old sins will rush in upon the believer's mind with a terrific force. Gathering dreadful strength from the justice of God, our eyes are tormented with the vision of an angry God, with His sword drawn, ready to smite us for our offenses. Glorious is that faith which can fling itself into the arms of God, even when the sword is in His hand, and will not believe that that God can strike the sinner who relies upon the blood of Jesus. Mighty is that faith which looking at justice, stern and severe, trembles not, but cries, "Thou art merciful and just to forgive me my sins, for I have confessed them. Christ hath full atonement made, and Thou wilt not twice demand the debt." Triumphant is that faith which marches right up to heaven, and stands before the blazing throne of the great and holy God, and yet can cry, "Who shall lay anything to the charge of God's elect?"

Brethren, be great believers. Little faith will bring your souls to heaven, but great faith will bring heaven to your souls.

7. The Work of the Holy Spirit

Spurgeon believed in the Personality of the Holy Spirit, and in His gracious working in the believer's heart and life. The activity of the Spirit of God was to him a vital reality which he felt mightily in his own labors in the bonds of the Gospel, and which gave vitality to all ministry, doctrine, and Christian experience. He affirmed that His divine work was absolutely essential in regeneration, sanctification, understanding the Word of God, and in the production of fruit in the graces of Christian character and service. He warned against grieving the Holy Spirit by sin, disobedience, unbelief, and backsliding.

> In the eternal covenant of grace the Holy Spirit was one of the high contracting parties in the divine contract, whereby we are saved. All that can be said of the love of the Father, of the love of the Son, may be said of the love of the Spirit—it is eternal, it is infinite, it is sovereign, it is everlasting.... Do you remember the love of the Spirit when, after having quickened you, He took you aside, and showed you Jesus on the tree? Who was it that opened your blind eyes to see a dying Savior? Who was it opened your deaf ear to hear the voice of pardoning love? Who opened your clasped and palsied hand to receive the tokens of a Savior's grace? Who was it that brake your hard heart and made a way for the Savior to enter and dwell therein? It was that precious Holy Spirit. We are but learners yet, unstable, weak and apt to slide, but what a blessed Instructor we have had! Has He not led us into many a truth, and taken of the things of Christ and applied them to us?

8. Holiness

Spurgeon constantly urged that the children of a holy God must themselves be holy, by the operation of the Holy Spirit and by maintaining a close and obedient walk with God. Sanctification to him was a threefold work of Father, Son, and Holy Spirit, which began in regeneration and went on as a continuing and ever deepening process throughout life, making a believer more godly and Christ-like until his entrance into heaven. He stood for a practical holiness which transformed and uplifted character, home life, business affairs, social duties, conversation, recreation and all that made up the life of man. This, of course, was a primary principle of the Puritans.

Holiness is the architectural plan on which God builds up His living temple. God has set apart His people from before the foundation of the world to be His chosen and peculiar inheritance. We are sanctified in Christ Jesus by the Holy Spirit when He subdues our corruptions, imparts to us grace, and leads us onward in the divine walk and life of faith. Christian men are not to be used for anything but God. They are a set-apart people; they are vessels of mercy, they are not for the devil's use, not for their own use, not for the world's use, but for their Master's use. He has made them on purpose to be used entirely, solely and wholly for Him. O Christian people, be holy, for Christ is holy. Do not pollute that holy Name wherewith you are named. Let your family life, your personal life, your business life, be as holy as Christ your Lord would have it to be. Shall saints be shams when sinners are so real?

9. *The Loveliness of Christ*

His heart filled with devotion and his face was radiant with delight as he spoke of the grace and love and beauty of his Lord. He wove rapturous thoughts from the Psalms and the Song of Solomon and the Epistles of Paul concerning the "Well-beloved." He delighted to speak of the person and work, the character and qualities of the Savior. From whatever text he took for his sermon he would soon make straight across country to the Lord Jesus. Christ was the golden key to Scripture for Spurgeon. He had no message whatever if he did not commend Christ and Him crucified and risen and exalted.

> Oh, how I love to hear Him praised! It sets my heart a-dancing. His name is sweet as the honeycomb, and His word is precious as the gold of Ophir (1 Kings 10:11). His person is very dear to us; from His head to His foot He is altogether lovely. When we get near Him, and see Him at the last, methinks we shall swoon away with excess of joy at the sight of Him; and I for one ask no heaven beyond a sight of Him and a smile of His love.

Especially in Christ's dying for sinners he saw the love of Christ and the loveliness of Christ.

> When a man can come right up to Christ and throw his arms around Him; when he can say, "That blood is mine: that Christ is my joy: His love is my love: His presence is my heaven: His character is my great example; I trust in Him, and I love Him"—he has said the thing that is essentially right, and his soul is safe.

> What was Jesus Christ to me at the first? He was the object of my warmest love; was it not with you also? Was He not chief among ten

thousand and the altogether lovely? What charms, what beauties were in that dear face of His. And what a freshness, what a novelty, what a delight, that set all our passions on a flame! It was so in those early days when we went after Him in the wilderness. Though all the world around was barren, He was all in all to us. What is He today? He is fairer to us now than ever He was. He is the one gem that we possess; our other jewels have all turned out to be but glass, but He is the *Koh-i-noor*[40] that our soul delights in; all perfections joined together to make one absolute perfection; all the graces adorning Him, and over-flowing to us.

10. The Final Perseverance of the Saints

In some ways this was the most precious of the doctrines of grace to Spurgeon. He constantly spoke of the eternal security of the believer. To him it was inconceivable that an elect and redeemed soul could finally fall away and be lost. He was convinced from Scripture that Christ's salvation was an eternal salvation. Yet he safeguarded the truth by insisting that the one way by which a soul will persevere to the end is by abiding in Christ.

> I cannot comprehend a gospel which lets saints fall away after they are called, and suffers the children of God to be burned in the fires of damnation after having believed in Jesus. If one dear saint of God had perished, so might all; if one of the covenant ones be lost, so may all be; and then there is no Gospel promise true, but the Bible is a lie, and there is nothing in it worth my acceptance. If God has loved me once, then He will love me for ever. God has a master-mind; He arranged everything in His gigantic intellect long before He did it: and once having settled it, He never alters it.

> *My name from the palms of His hands*
> *Eternity will not erase;*
> *Impressed on His heart it remains,*
> *In marks of indelible grace.*

Indelible grace!

If I did not believe the doctrine of the final perseverance of the saints I think I should be of all men the most miserable, because I should lack

---

40. An Indian diamond weighing 106 carats—now part of the British crown jewels; a Persian term which literally means "mountain of light."

any ground of comfort.

If you, believer in Christ, are the most obscure of all the family, you shall never perish. If you have indeed received the inner life and true grace by Christ in thy soul, though no one knows your name, and no one lends you a helping hand; though as a solitary pilgrim you should walk the heavenly road all alone, weak and feeble—yet you shall never perish! Christ's sheep were of old chosen of God unto salvation; but if they perished the election of God would be frustration. The purpose of God secures their final perseverance. We may rest assured that they shall be preserved because of the effectual redemption Christ wrought for them. If He has borne their punishment, they have no penalty to suffer. How shall the man that believes in Christ be condemned for the sin that has been pardoned? In the believer, moreover, there is a work of God begun which He has engaged to complete. It hath never been said of God that He began to build and was not able to finish.

We have cause for great watchfulness, deep humility, but also much thankfulness, for the promise assures us that none is able to pluck us out of Christ's hand. The destroyer has never yet celebrated a triumph over the Redeemer. He is not able to hold up a single jewel of the Redeemer's crown and say, "Aha! Aha! I stole it from thy diadem. You could not keep it!" It cannot be; it *shall* not be.... There is Christ's hand, and His people in it, and He shall shut it fast to hold them. But, then, that hand was pierced once, and so to make it doubly sure the Father clasps it with His hand, and so within a double enclosure the elect of God are held and embraced. There is the pierced hand of Jesus, and there is the Father's Almighty hand—two hands to protect and defend them. They must, they *shall,* for ever rest in perfect security beneath the guardian care of the Mediator, Christ the Lord, and God the Everlasting and Ever-blessed Father" (John 10:27-30).

11. The Return of the Lord

The Second Advent of Christ was preached by Spurgeon throughout his entire ministry. He believed, on the authority of the Word of God, that Christ Jesus would one day return to earth literally, corporally, visibly, in power and great glory. He delighted to set this forth as the blessed hope and glory of the Church, and to call his people to preparedness and watchfulness for their returning King. He did not preach this doctrine as some do today, as an "any moment" and "secret" coming. Nor did he attempt the fixing of dates, as others do, although he did set forth what he believed to be Scriptural signs of Christ's appearing. He ever emphasized the fact of the Lord's return, and its great consequences for the believer, the Church, and the world. He was assured from Scripture that at His coming Christ would complete and glorify His church, establish His millennial kingdom, punish his foes, and destroy Satan and all his works. He would also unite in one glorious host all his saints, those who slept until the first resurrection, and those on the earth at His Advent.

> That same Jesus Who went up from Olivet into heaven is coming again to earth in like manner as His disciples saw Him go up into heaven. We have His own word for it, and this makes assurance doubly sure. Moreover, the great scheme of redemption requires Christ's return. It is a part of that scheme that as He came once with a sin-offering to redeem, so He should come a second time without a sin-offering to claim the inheritance that He has so dearly bought. He came once that His heel might be bruised; He comes again to bruise the serpent's head, and with a rod of iron to dash his enemies in pieces as potter's vessels. He came once to wear the crown of thorns; He must come again to wear the diadem of universal dominion. He comes to the marriage supper. He comes to gather His saints together. He comes to glorify them with Himself on this same earth where once He and they were despised and rejected of men. The whole drama of redemption cannot be perfected without this last act of the coming of the King.

Spurgeon's theology can be summed up in one word—*Christ-centered*. In his first sermon in the Metropolitan Tabernacle he had said: "I would propose that the subject of the ministry of this house shall be the Person of Jesus Christ, the only mediator between God and man ... in the solitariness of His redemptive work, and as the sole King of His church." His last words in his pulpit, on Sunday morning, June 7, 1891, were:

> Jesus Christ is the most magnanimous of Captains. There never was His like among the choicest of princes. The heaviest end of the Cross lies ever on His shoulders. If there is anything that is gracious, generous, kind and tender, yea lavish and superabundant in love, you always find it in Him! His service is life, peace, joy. Oh that you would enter it at once! *God help you to enlist under the banner of Jesus Christ!*

The Puritans were Christ-centered men. Their thoughts and hopes, their teachings and ways were all associated with the Son of God, all regulated and controlled by His grace and truth and will. So it was with

Spurgeon. He had nothing to say if he could not speak of Jesus. The deep reality of the presence and power of Christ molded his whole life and ministry. The Son of God was everything to him. Theology was a poor second. "I love those five points (of Calvinism)," he said, "as being the angles of the Gospel, but then I love the Center between the angles better still." In his diary for April 12, 1850, he wrote: "Earthly things have engaged too much of my thoughts this day. I have not been able to fix my thoughts entirely upon my Savior. I would be ever with Thee, O my spotless, fairest Beloved! Daily meet me, for Thy embrace is Heaven; sanctify me, prepare me, help me to bring forth fruit and to be Thine forever!" The prayer was abundantly answered. His pulpit prayers often expressed a rapture of adoration and devotion directed towards his Well-beloved. With Spurgeon, Christ was never far from his thoughts or conversation. With him it was Jesus always, and Jesus only! Once, in Rome, he climbed to the top of the Coliseum, looked at the arena where Christians had died for their faith, and then began to sing:

> *I'm not ashamed to own my Lord,*
> *Or to defend His cause;*
> *Maintain the honour of His word,*
> *The glory of His cross.*

In one of Spurgeon's travelogue lectures he ended thus:

> If you cannot travel, remember that our Lord Jesus Christ is more glorious than all else that you could ever see. Get a view of Christ, and you have seen more than mountains and cascades and valleys and seas can ever show you. Earth may give its beauty, and stars their brightness, but all these put together can never rival Him.

Christ was the secret of his power.

Spurgeon's opinion of the Puritans, with whom he was acquainted in his childhood, and to whom he owed so much all his days, never changed. In 1872 he said:

> We assert this day that, when we take down a volume of Puritan theology, we find in a solitary page more thinking and more learning, more Scripture, more real teaching, than in whole folios of the effusions of modern thought. The modern men would be rich if they possessed even the crumbs that fall from the table of the Puritans.

Chapter 11
Mr. Valiant-for-Truth

We both fight and prevail in the power of His might.... In all, especially difficult encounters, let us lift up our hearts to Christ, Who has Spirit enough for us all.... There can be no victory where there is no combat. The victory lies not upon us but upon Christ, Who hath taken upon Him, as to conquer for us, so to conquer in us. Let us not look so much who are our enemies, as Who is our Judge and Captain; not what they threaten, but what He promises.

—RICHARD SIBBES, *THE BRUISED REED*

In all the wonderful picture gallery of Bunyan's *Pilgrim's Progress* there is no finer portrait than that of Mr. Valiant-for-Truth. We first meet him with his sword drawn in his hand, and with blood upon his face, he having put to flight three robbers. He was, he tells us, born in Darkland, and after a wonderful conversion was on his way to the Celestial City. Like Christian he had many terrible and dangerous experiences to pass through, but he got the victory for his was "a right Jerusalem blade." Valiant-for-Truth was a singer also, and sang; right lustily:

> *Who would true Valour see,*
> *Let him come hither;*
> *One here will constant be,*
> *Come Wind, come Weather.*
> *There's no discouragement*
> *Shall make him once Relent*
> *His first avow'd Intent*
> *To be a Pilgrim.*

When the summons came to this stalwart soldier of the Cross he called for his friends and told them of it.

Then said he: "I am going to my Fathers, and though with great difficulty I am got hither, yet now I do not repent me of all the trouble I have been at to arrive where I am. My sword I give to him that shall succeed me in my pilgrimage, and my courage and skill to him that can get it. My marks and scars I carry with me to be a witness for me that I have fought His battles Who will be my Rewarder." When the day that he must go hence was come, many accompanied him to the River side, into which as he went he said: "Death, where is thy sting?" And as he went deeper he said: "Grave, where is thy victory?" So he passed over, and all the trumpets sounded for him on the other side.

Charles Haddon Spurgeon was a true Mr. Valiant-for-Truth. His sword was a "right Jerusalem blade" also, the Word of God which he well knew how to wield, and by means of which he dealt many shrewd blows against the hosts of darkness.

Although he had no love of controversy for its own sake, yet as he said in 1864, "When the gage of battle is thrown down, I am not the man to refuse to take it up." No, indeed! During his lifetime he engaged in two great controversies—one concerning baptismal regeneration; the other concerning the orthodoxy of ministers and churches, the famous "Down Grade" controversy. Some of Spurgeon's biographers have sought to minimize these, or even to ignore them altogether, but they were of great importance in his life and no adequate account of his ministry is possible that does not give due weight to them. What contribution did they make to the explication of truth or the furtherance of the Kingdom? We have read much on both controversies from writers on both sides, and trust that the various matters involved will be fairly and justly treated so that the reader may come to his own satisfactory conclusion.

BAPTISMAL REGENERATION

The Baptismal Regeneration controversy burst unexpectedly on a slumbering religious world in 1864. On June 5th, in his own pulpit at the Metropolitan Tabernacle, Spurgeon preached a sermon on the text, "Go ye into all the world and preach the Gospel to every creature. He that believeth and is baptised shall be saved; and he that believeth not shall be damned" (Mark 16:15-16). It was a very long sermon, and it was a terrific attack upon what he regarded as superstition sanctioned in Protestant churches under traditional and accepted views of the meaning and effects of infant baptism. Spurgeon was a convinced Baptist from the time of his conversion. When he republished the Puritan classic, Thomas Watson's *Body of Divinity,* he added an "Appendix on Baptism" to refute the beloved Puritan's paedo-Baptist views. But Watson, of course, did not believe in baptismal regeneration. In 1864 Spurgeon's opponents were the High Church and Sacerdotal party in the Church of England. He also directed his attacks on the wording of the *Book of Common Prayer* in several places. The sermon was not, in fact, an attack on infant baptism but on the doctrine of baptismal regeneration.

He told his hearers that the burden of the Lord was upon him and he must deliver his soul. He was, he said, forced by "an awful and overwhelming sense of duty." Then he plunged into the fray, striking out right, left, and center with his "right Jerusalem sword." Strong arguments, and strong words, followed.

The error of baptismal regeneration, he contended, was in direct opposition to his text. Baptism without faith saved no one. The Church of England—"this very powerful sect," he called it—clearly taught the doctrine openly, boldly and plainly in the *Book of Common Prayer.* He proceeded to quote the Church's Catechism in which it is stated that by baptism a young person is "made a member of Christ, a child of God, and an inheritor of the Kingdom of Heaven." Those phrases, he urged, had no meaning and were untrue for those who had no faith. Next, the words in the Baptism service came under review: "Seeing now, dearly beloved brethren, that this child is regenerate and grafted into the body of Christ's Church, let us give thanks unto Almighty God for these benefits…." He strongly denied the truth of these words, and claimed that Evangelical clergy in the Church of England who did not themselves believe in baptismal regeneration were committing perjury by using them. They took money, he said, for defending what they did not believe, and their action tended to debauch the public mind.

This was strong stuff indeed. Spurgeon went on to argue against the notion that people were saved by baptism. It was out of character with the spiritual religion of Christ. It was on a par with the prayer-windmills of Tibet and the superstition of Pilate's staircase in Rome. The dogma was not supported by facts, for all the baptized were clearly not the children of God. Thousands of the baptized were in prison, some had even been hanged, while others were drunkards, whoremongers and fornicators. "The performance styled baptism by the Prayer Book is not at all likely to regenerate and save," he said.

He went on to describe the service at the font, and urged how impossible it was for the parents and godparents, even if truly godly persons, to renounce on behalf of the child what they found it hard to renounce for themselves—"the devil and all his works, the vain pomp and glory of the world ... and the carnal desires of the flesh." He declared that it was an encouragement to Popery, and cried, "We want John Knox back again!" That baptism saved the soul was the most atrocious lie that had dragged millions down to hell! Faith was the indispensable requirement for salvation which was the work of the Holy Spirit and the gift of God. The baptism spoken of in the text was evidently connected with faith. Salvation was not by baptism, he concluded, but by the blood of Christ.

The printed sermon sold no less than a quarter of a million copies. To say that the sermon caused a sensation is an understatement. It let loose a storm against him by many in the Church of England. A war of pamphlets and sermons followed in which many telling points were made, and in which Spurgeon was attacked or defended, but very often the main thesis—the superstition of the doctrine of baptismal regeneration was overlooked. Spurgeon's friend, the Rev. W. Landels of Regent's Park Chapel, joined in, and so did the Rev. W. Goode, Dean of Ripon. Dean Goode expressed himself thus:

> As to that young minister who is now raving against the Evangelical clergy on this point, it is to be regretted that so much notice has been taken of his railings. He is to be pitied, because his entire want of acquaintance with theological literature leaves him utterly unfit for the determination of such a question, which is a question not of mere doctrine, but of what may be called historical theology.... Let him hold and enforce his own view of doctrine as he pleases; but when he undertakes to determine what is the exclusive meaning of the *Book of Common Prayer*, and brings a charge of dishonesty against those who take a different view of that meaning from what he does, he only shows the presumptuous self-confidence with which he is prepared to pronounce judgment upon matters of which he is profoundly ignorant. To hold a controversy with him upon the subject would be to as little purpose as to attempt to hold a logically-constructed argument with a child unacquainted with logical terms.

Perhaps it was the Dean who was a little ignorant. "Entire want of acquaintance with theological literature..."? Surely not, with all those hundreds of volumes in his library, William Cunningham's *Historical Theology* published in 1862 among them!

Spurgeon in his study

Some of the pamphlets of Spurgeon's era had intriguing titles—in the best vein of the seventeenth century Puritans—such as *An Artful Fox Unearthed and Trapped* by R. A. Bellman, of which 7,000 were sold. The same author, warming to his work, wrote *Great is Diana, or Mother Church and the Babes*, with a sale of 15,000. Later on he came out with *Curious Twistings; or the Contortions or Distortions of the Rev. R. P. Hutchinston*, BA (5,000 copies). Other brethren contributed to the discussion pamphlets entitled, *Regeneration or Degeneration; Clerical Logic Illustrated; Clerical Shuffling; and The Tables Turned.*

Spurgeon returned to the attack with further sermons. On June 16th the subject was "Let us go forth therefore unto Him without the camp, bearing His reproach." In this he spoke of the Church of England as:

> ... a Church which tolerates Evangelical truth in her communion, but at the same time lovingly embraces Puseyism,[41] and finds room for infidels and for men who deny the authenticity of Scripture. This is no

time for us to talk about friendship with so corrupt a corporation. The godly in her midst are deceived if they think to mold her to a more gracious form.... Flee out of her all ye who love your souls!

This, not unnaturally, enraged many clergy still more.

On July 24th he preached from Mark 10:13-16 the incident of the young children brought to Jesus. The printed sermon was headed, "Children Brought to Christ, Not to the Font."[42] He pointed out that the passage in question had no connection whatever with baptism. The object was for Christ to touch them. The disciples did not baptize infants. Jesus Himself did not baptize children or say one word about baptismal regeneration. "Faith is the way to Jesus; baptism is not." He urged them to labor for the conversion of children in every way possible.

On September 25th Spurgeon had more to say on the subject. Preaching on the text, "Thus saith the Lord," Ezekiel 11:5, the sermon had the bold title, "Thus saith the Lord, or The Book of Common Prayer Weighed in the Balances of the Sanctuary." After asserting the authority of Scripture in all matters of faith, he proceeded to examine various parts of the Prayer Book. Once again he denounced the wording of the infant baptism service. It seemed to him that the godparents might just as well promise that the infants should grow up with Roman noses, auburn hair, and blue eyes, as that they should renounce the devil and all his works. The Lord nowhere said that an unconscious babe by water baptism was made a member of Christ or a child of God. He then turned to the Confirmation service, and denied that the bishop could certify divine favor towards those on whom his hands were laid. He examined the priest's absolution for the sick, and questioned his right to say, "I absolve thee from all thy sins." The service for "The Ordering of Priests" was likewise weighed in the balances and found wanting. The bishop had no power to give those ordained the Holy Spirit. He also denied that Queen Victoria was Head of the Church—this caused a fresh rumpus!—and concluded by roundly condemning certain Church of England canons ... NO. 10, "Maintainers of Schismatics [or Divisions] in the Church of England to be cen-

---

41. Referring to Dr. Pusey, the Tractarian leader.

42. A receptacle, or bowl-like vessel, placed on a pedestal for the water used in baptism; the term is derived from the Latin word for *fountain*.

sured"; and NO. 11, "Maintainers of Conventicles[43] censured." If any of these matters did not stand the test of "Thus saith the Lord," then they must be rejected.

The war of sermons and pamphlets continued. Mr. Bellman added more fuel to the fire. Newspapers seized on juicy tidbits to amaze their readers. Anglican pulpit thundered against Baptist pulpit; the chapel and meeting-house spoke sharply to parish church and cathedral. There was a vast amount of verbosity, and as in most controversies everyone was persuaded by his own arguments, and none were convinced by those of the opposite side.

Spurgeon was a member of The Evangelical Alliance, composed of both Anglicans and Free Churchmen, but the criticism of some Anglican members caused him to resign. Later on he rejoined, and found much support from many of them in the "Down Grade" controversy.

What was achieved? Very little. The advocates of baptismal regeneration continued on their way. Anglican Evangelicals maintained their interpretation of the word "regeneration" in the Prayer Book. Baptists took heart and were strengthened in their faith. Dr. W. Y. Fullerton says that the whole affair was a statement of futility. Spurgeon thought that he was battling for vital truth, and was blithely unconcerned as to what men said of him. He reveled in the battle almost joyously. It was far different in the later controversy.

THE DOWN GRADE CONTROVERSY

The second great controversy in which Spurgeon was involved, the "Down Grade" controversy of 1887-1889, was of an altogether different stamp. It concerned questions of fundamental importance; it had profound consequences lasting even down to our own day. It must be regarded as one of the major crises in English church history during the last century.

Several accounts have been written of this dispute. Drs. W. Y. Fullerton and J. C. Carlile in their *Lives of Spurgeon;* Dr. A. C. Underwood in his *History of the English Baptists* (an eminently fair record); Dr. Ernest A. Payne in *The Baptist Union: A Short History* (the official Baptist Union version); and the Rev. E. J. Poole-Connor in *Evangelicalism in*

---

43. "Conventicles" is a term derived from the Latin which refers to places of meeting or assembly, especially Nonconformist meeting houses.

England. This latter book is of great value as it draws on the writings of the Rev. Henry Oakley who was present at the Assembly of 1888.

When these various accounts are compared it is obvious that there are considerable differences between them, not only as to the actual facts of the case, but also regarding the interpretation of the facts. Many who wrote did so on behalf of one side or the other, and at this distance of time it is not easy to get at the truth. However, we have earnestly endeavored to give a fair and just account of the whole matter so far as it can now be ascertained.

The question at issue was the orthodoxy or otherwise of ministers and churches in the Baptist denomination. It was a real defense of the faith on Spurgeon's part, as the other controversy was not. He was much older, more mature, and more restrained in speech. Some of his opponents have urged that his attitudes were caused by his ill-health. It is true that his health was poor, but his mental grasp of the issues involved was clear and piercing, and his heart was as bold as a lion. Mr. Valiant-for-Truth indeed.

It is surprising how quietly the whole affair began. From different quarters Spurgeon began to hear of odd, unscriptural things being preached in Baptist pulpits. For instance, at Upper Norwood Baptist Chapel, quite near his own home, the minister, Dr. S. A. Tipple, was preaching sermons on "Parables from Nature." They were published, and Spurgeon said that they had not enough Gospel in them to save a cat! He had, of course, many friends in all parts of the country, a large number trained in the ministry in the Pastors' College, and these began to report to him of various preachers regarded as unsound in the faith. There had been for some time a growing departure from Calvinistic doctrine and vital Evangelical emphases on the part of many ministers. The divine inspiration of Scripture, the Virgin Birth of our Lord, the substitutionary atonement of Christ, the reality of heaven and hell, were some of the doctrines regarded by Spurgeon as of vital importance that were being denied or interpreted in a latitudinarian sense. The impact of the Higher Criticism of the Scriptures and of the rationalistic theology from Germany associated with the names of J. G. Eichorn, Wellhausen, and Robertson Smith in Britain, began to be manifest in the theological colleges and among the ministry. The theory of biological evolution associated with the name of Charles Darwin invaded the minds of many and appeared to dethrone a Creator, and make a plan of salvation unnecessary.

Even the Secretary of the Baptist Union, Dr. S. H. Booth, was disturbed, quite independently of Spurgeon be it noted, concerning some men and things in the denomination. He had already been involved in an inquiry into the orthodoxy of the Rev. W. E. Blomfield of Beckenham, who was exonerated at the time, and later became Principal of Rawdon Baptist College. Names mentioned to both Booth and Spurgeon included J. G. Greenhough, James Thew, Dr. S. Cox, and Dr. S. A. Tipple among others. Dr. Underwood says, "Many wrote to Spurgeon pleading with him to do something to stem the tide of 'modern thought.'"

Sometime during the summer of 1887, Dr. Booth wrote to Spurgeon for advice. He was alarmed at the public utterances of some members of the Baptist Union Council, and felt that they should be called to account. Unfortunately there was no machinery in the Union by which this could be done. The character of the theological teaching given in some of the Baptist Colleges also alarmed him. He gave Spurgeon the names and extracts from the sermons and speeches of which he complained.

About the same time Spurgeon's magazine, *The Sword and Trowel*, printed two unsigned articles entitled "The Down Grade," drawing attention to the ways in which unsound doctrine and heresy can obtain a foothold in the churches. Many jumped to the conclusion that the author was Spurgeon himself, but in fact the articles came from the pen of the Rev. Robert Shindler. Undoubtedly Spurgeon agreed wholeheartedly with the writer and his conclusions, although there is no evidence that he inspired the articles. Many in the churches greatly rejoiced that a voice had been raised against unorthodoxy and liberalism.

In the magazine for August 1887, Spurgeon wrote a signed article entitled "Another Word Concerning the Down Grade." In this he declared:

> The Atonement is rejected, the inspiration of Scripture is derided, the Holy Spirit is degraded into an influence, the punishment of sin is turned into a fiction, and the resurrection into a myth, and yet these enemies of our faith expect us to call them brethren and maintain a confederacy with them.

In September he wrote, "A Reply to Sundry Critics and Inquirers."

We have received abundant proofs that our alarm was none too soon. Letters from all quarters declare that the case of the church at this present is worse than we thought it to be.... A chasm is opening.... Let us take our places, not in anger nor in the spirit of suspicion or division, but in watchfulness and resolve.

He went on:

Inspiration and speculation cannot long abide in peace. Compromise there can be none. We cannot hold the inspiration of the Word, and yet reject it; we cannot believe in the atonement and deny it; we cannot hold the doctrine of the fall and yet talk of the evolution of spiritual life from human nature; we cannot recognize the punishment of the impenitent and yet indulge the "larger hope." One way or the other we must go. Decision is the virtue of the hour.

In October he concluded the series of articles with one entitled "The Case Proved." But was it? He thought so. He also charged that certain ministers had initiated "a new religion, which was no more Christianity than chalk was cheese." The articles were widely read and discussed throughout the denomination and beyond on the eve of the Autumn meetings of the Baptist Union at Sheffield in October. Spurgeon hoped that Dr. Booth, the Secretary, would initiate some definite action at that Assembly, and was upset when nothing transpired. On the other hand, Spurgeon though hitherto a warm friend of the Union, an attendant at its gatherings, and often a preacher at its meetings, had sent no communication on the matter in order to raise the issue. It probably would have been better had he done so.

Booth and Spurgeon were undoubtedly in close contact on the issue at this time; letters passed between them, and it is most likely that they met together to discuss so vital a matter. Spurgeon wanted the Baptist Union to issue a declaration clearly stating the Evangelical beliefs of the denomination along the lines of the doctrinal basis of the Evangelical Alliance. This surely was a sound suggestion, and would have placed the Union in a position of strength with which to deal with the situation and confront those who deviated from the truth. But the Baptist Union took the line that the denomination as a whole was against creedal statements and insisted on liberty to interpret doctrine as they were led. But what if they were being led in a wrong direction ... or downhill? Spurgeon and his friends were convinced that they were. There was, of course, no reason why the Baptists should not have issued a statement of their faith. They had often before done so: in 1677 there was a Particular Baptist Confession, and in 1678 The General Baptist Confession; and there were others of later date.

The Press was full of rumors. *The Scotsman* printed a report "on the most trustworthy authority" that Spurgeon had "intimated his intention of withdrawing from the Union if certain ministers whom he considers heretical—notably Mr. Greenhough of Leicester—are not expelled." Spurgeon's secretary issued an unqualified contradiction. The Baptist paper *The Freeman* published a facetious paragraph in which the "Down Grade" question was described as "a great joke." This seriously wounded Spurgeon, and later an apology was printed by the paper for this statement.

In the preface to the 1887 volume of sermons, Spurgeon wrote:

> Something will come of the struggle over the "Down Grade." The Lord has designs in connection therewith which His adversaries little dream of. Meanwhile, it behooves all who love the Lord Jesus to keep close together, and make common cause against deadly error. There are thousands who are of one mind in the Lord; let them break through all the separating lines of sect, and show their unity in Christ, both by prayer and action.

Dr. David Brown, Principal of the Free Church College, Aberdeen, wrote in *The Sword and Trowel* of those who:

> ... are expected to preach the faith of orthodox Christendom ... yet neither hold nor teach that faith, but do their best to undermine the sacred records of it. I should not have said so much were it not that all our churches were honeycombed with this mischievous tendency to minimize all those features of the Gospel the natural man cannot receive.

Not less to the point was a quotation given by *The Sword and Trowel* from the current issue of *The Christian World,* one of Spurgeon's most outspoken antagonists. So far from denying the prevalence of "modern thought" its editor exulted in it, and taunted those who endeavored to conceal the facts. He wrote:

> Modern thought is in Mr. Spurgeon's eyes a "deadly cobra"; in ours it is the glory of the century. It discards many of the doctrines dear to Mr. Spurgeon and his school, not only as untrue and unscriptural, but as in the strictest sense immoral. It is not so irrational as to pin its faith to verbal inspiration, nor so idolatrous as to make its acceptance of a true Trinity cover polytheism.

Dr. John Clifford now entered the lists with an article in the *Pall Mall Gazette,* edited by W. T. Stead. He was Vice President of the Baptist

Union in 1887 and president in the crucial year 1888. A decided modernist or liberal in theology, he was, on the whole, more concerned with a social gospel than with the salvation of sinners. His election to the presidency had been strenuously opposed by the Rev. James Douglas, MA, of Brixton, one of Spurgeon's friends, who said, "I must place in the foreground the faith once delivered to the saints. I do not look upon Dr. Clifford as a sufficient exponent of that faith for the office of Vice President." Spurgeon counted Clifford as one of his friends in spite of their differences in theology, and, according to Sir William Robertson Nicoll, declined to rank him among the heretics. Clifford wrote that Spurgeon's statements were unproved, and in his opinion unprovable; that the Baptist ministry was sounder than ever, and that nothing had been shed but "metaphysical conceptions of medieval philosophy."

Spurgeon, finding that no headway could be made, withdrew from the Baptist Union in October 1887. His letter of resignation was in the following terms:

> *Dear Friend,*
>
> *I beg to intimate to you, as Secretary of the Baptist Union, that I must withdraw from that Society. I do this with the utmost regret, but I have no choice. The reasons are set forth in The Sword and Trowel for November, and I trust you will excuse my repeating them here. I beg you not to send anyone to me to ask for a reconsideration. I fear I have considered too long already. Certainly every hour of the day impresses upon me the conviction that I am moving none too soon. I wish to add that no personal bitterness or ill-will in the least degree has overcome me. I have personally received more respect than I desire. It is on the highest grounds alone that I take this step, and you know that I have delayed it because I hoped for better things.*
>
> *Yours always heartily,*
> *C. H. Spurgeon.*

Booth, greatly surprised and alarmed, replied as follows:

I cannot express adequately the sense of pain such a step has caused me. Nor can I, at present, calmly think of the future. I can only leave it as it is for a while, merely adding that I think you have wounded the hearts of some—of many—who honor and love you more than you have any idea of, and whose counsel would have led to a far different result.

This last notion is odd. Did Booth think that Spurgeon had not consulted his friends and taken their counsel? He had been in anxious communication with them for months. His resignation had been no hasty step but one of long considered and prayerful thought. Spurgeon was followed in withdrawing from the Baptist Union by James Douglas, Archibald Brown, Robert Shindler and others, including his own son Charles, but not his brother James. The Metropolitan Tabernacle and some other churches also left the Union. Dr. Payne points out how difficult it was for ordinary ministers to leave the Baptist Union since their incomes were augmented by Baptist Union funds, without which they would have been in serious difficulties. Sympathize with Spurgeon they might, but resign with him, no.

The press seized upon Spurgeon's resignation as headline news. *John Bull* had an article entitled "The Decomposition of Dissent." *The Pall Mall Gazette* printed a long reply by Dr. Clifford to Spurgeon's *Sword and Trowel* articles. *The British Weekly, Christian World,* and *The Freeman* all joined in the fray with gusto, expressing regret at Spurgeon's action and sympathy with the Baptist Union. Public meetings to air the issues involved were held in various places.

In November, Spurgeon wrote in his magazine:

> Believers in Christ's atonement are now in declared union with those who make light of it; believers in Holy Scripture are in confederacy with those who deny plenary inspiration; those who hold Evangelical doctrine are in open alliance with those who call the Fall a fable, who deny the personality of the Holy Ghost, who call justification by faith, immoral, and hold that there is another probation after death.... Yes, we have before us the wretched spectacle of professedly orthodox Christians publicly avowing their union with those who deny the faith, and scarcely concealing their contempt for those who cannot be guilty of such gross disloyalty to Christ. To be plain, we are unable to call these things Christian Unions, they begin to look like Confederacies in Evil.... It is our solemn conviction that where there can be no real spiritual communion there should be no pretense of fellowship. *Fellowship with known and vital error is participation in sin.*

This last sentence, which we have italicized, was the very heart and center of Spurgeon's whole testimony in the matter. He refused to be connected with men who taught error or half-truths or who, in his view, denied fundamental Bible doctrines.

The Council of the Baptist Union met in December 1887 to deliberate on the crisis in its ranks. Eighty out of one hundred members were present. It seems to have been a somewhat confused gathering by all accounts. Dr. Angus submitted a declaration of Evangelical faith, specifying certain doctrinal tenets and affirming confidence in the Evangelical soundness of the denomination. Spurgeon's brother James proposed that the Union should adopt the doctrinal basis of the Evangelical Alliance. Discussion of both motions was deferred. James Spurgeon reported that it was "a horrible meeting." Many thought that Spurgeon should be interviewed despite his expressed unwillingness, and it was decided that a deputation should meet him, if necessary at Mentone where he was recuperating after illness.

Spurgeon wrote to Dr. Booth to say that he felt that he must now hand over to the Council of the Union the letters which had passed between them and which contained specific charges against certain unorthodox ministers. This was a perfectly proper attitude to take, and one which would have cleared Spurgeon of many of the accusations leveled against him to the effect that his criticisms were vague and nebulous. But Dr. Booth replied that his correspondence with Spurgeon was not official but confidential, and that Spurgeon could not in honor use it. From this it is obvious that Spurgeon's hands were tied, and that the responsibility for the subsequent unfortunate proceedings rests squarely with Booth.

Dr. J. C. Carlile says:

> Spurgeon was never righted. The impression still remains in many quarters that he made charges which could not be substantiated, and that when called upon to produce the evidence he resigned and ran away. Nothing could be further from the truth. Spurgeon could have produced Dr. Booth's letters. I think he should have done so.

The great preacher's health was beginning to fail, and he was away at Mentone in the South of France, recuperating. On his return home in January 1888 he met a deputation from the Baptist Union at the Metropolitan Tabernacle, consisting of Drs. Culross, Clifford, and Booth. James Spurgeon was with his brother. It was not an easy meeting, and matters had gone too far for an immediate reconciliation. To Spurgeon the very heart and existence of the Evangelical Faith in the Baptist denomination was at stake. He refused to withdraw his resignation, and again pressed the Union to adopt a doctrinal declaration similar to that of the Evangelical Alliance which would affirm, once for all, the theological position of Baptists on vital points of truth. Moreover, he declined to give the names of the unorthodox because the Baptist Union had no power over them, and because there was no machinery under the Baptist Union Constitution for dealing with divergencies of doctrine. In addition, as Dr. Booth would not allow the letters between them to pass into the hands of the Council it was impossible for him to name persons and go into details concerning their alleged errors.

In a sermon at the Tabernacle about this time, Spurgeon said:

> Suppose the Church at large should decline to a spiritual death—and I am sure it does so just now—what then? The faults which are now so apparent may only be the beginning of worse evils. Suppose error should become rampant in all our churches, as it may; suppose those who bear testimony should grow fewer, and their voices should be less and less regarded, as they may be; suppose at last the true Church of Christ should scarcely be discoverable, and that men should bury it, and dance a saraband[44] upon its grave, and say, "We have done with these believers in atonement. We have done with these troublesome Evangelical doctrines." What then? The truth will rise again. The eternal Gospel will burst her sepulchre. "Vain the watch, the stone, the seal."

The Baptist Union Council met again on January 15, 1888, and passed a resolution accepting Spurgeon's resignation. Another resolution was then brought forward as follows:

> That the Council recognizes the gravity of the charges which Mr. Spurgeon has brought against the Union previous to and since his withdrawal. It considers that the public and general manner in which they have been made reflects on the whole body, and exposes to suspicion brethren who love the truth as dearly as he does. And, as Mr. Spurgeon declined to give the names of those to whom he intended them to apply, and the evidence supporting them, those charges in the judgment of the Council, ought not to have been made.

---

44. A graceful, stately, slow Spanish dance.

This resolution was moved by William Landels, of Regent's Park Chapel, who had been a close friend of Spurgeon, and was passed with only five dissenters, one of whom was James Spurgeon. One of the speakers was J. G. Greenhough, widely regarded as one of the chief deviationists from Scriptural doctrine, who presented a "confession of faith" expressed in somewhat general terms. This vote of censure on Spurgeon, as it came to be called, roused much resentment among Spurgeon's friends, especially as several Evangelical members of the Council, who shared Spurgeon's alarm at the departure of many from the biblical faith, supported it. Dr. W. Y. Fullerton describes the resolution as "more worthy of a pettifogging lawyer, a peevish woman, or a petulant child, than of a body of high-minded men." To Spurgeon the issue was crystal clear. As he said, "Shall the Baptist Union be a resort for men of every school of thought, or shall it be declared to be an Evangelical institution?" Time, alas, has shown that it is the former conception which has prevailed.

In February, the Council of the Baptist Union met again to consider a Declaration of Faith prepared by Dr. Angus. It was much criticized by S. G. Green, J. G. Greenhough and others, and eventually agreed to with a preamble suggested by Dr. Clifford as follows:

> First, that the doctrinal beliefs of the Union are and must be determined by the doctrinal beliefs of the churches and Associations of which the Union is composed. Secondly, that the Council of the Union therefore disclaims altogether any authority to formulate a new and additional standard of theological belief as a bond of union to which assent shall be required.

This preamble was accepted by James Spurgeon, and the Council assumed that his acceptance carried with it that of Charles Haddon Spurgeon. But surely nothing could more clearly demonstrate the weakness of the Baptist Union position than this preamble. It was quite insufficient to rely on the beliefs of *the churches and Associations* which were subject to modification, and even then were changing fast. Indeed, in many cases their beliefs had never been formulated in any adequate way. The only firm basis for faith, and the standard of testing it, was the Holy Scriptures to which Spurgeon appealed. The Baptist Union gave its whole case away by setting up the notions of men as the standard instead of the inspired Word of God. But they did not seem to realize it. They were determined to justify themselves at all costs. And, be it noted, although they wrangled about the business, they did not pray about it! Spurgeon and his students held prayer meetings.

The Pastors' College Conference sent a protest to the Union against the vote of censure. So also did a number of ministers and churches.

The crucial drama of the "Down Grade" controversy now took place. The Baptist Union Assembly met in April 1888 at The City Temple, London, under the Presidency of Dr. John Clifford. The church was crammed to the doors. "A Declaratory Statement of facts and principles commonly believed by churches in the Union" was before the Assembly for acceptance or rejection. After a passage concerning believers' baptism and the Lord's Supper, it set forth six doctrines "commonly believed." They were: (1) the Divine Inspiration and Authority of the Holy Scriptures, (2) the fallen and sinful state of man, (3) the Person and Work of Jesus Christ, (4) Justification by Faith, (5) the Work of the Holy Spirit, (6) the Resurrection and the Judgment at the Last Day, "according to the words of our Lord in Matthew 24:46."

Now, on the surface, several of these would appear to be such as Spurgeon himself would accept. But on closer examination it is plain that they are stated in most general terms, and several are capable of widely different interpretations. Further, nothing whatever is said of the Substitutionary Atonement of Christ, the Virgin Birth, the Holy Trinity, Sanctification, or the Second Advent of Christ. The phrase Justification by Faith has the vital word "only" omitted.

The resolution was moved by the Rev. Charles Williams of Accrington, an advocate of advanced theology and hostile to Spurgeon, and it was seconded by James Spurgeon. Williams lost no time in making it clear that he spoke as one defending liberal theology, and repudiating Spurgeon's protests. It was a wily and bitter speech, and James Spurgeon's first words on rising to speak was that he seconded the motion but not the mover's speech! James Spurgeon's position in the whole affair was a curious one. He was not so conservative in his outlook as his brother (he had been trained at Regent's Park College under Dr. Angus), and he endeavored to mediate between the Baptist Union and Charles. He did not succeed in this, and he did not leave the Union. His attitude was undoubtedly a keen disappointment to Spurgeon. Writing to a friend, Spurgeon said: "My brother thinks he has gained a great victory, but I believe we are hopelessly sold. I feel heartbroken. Certainly he has done the opposite of what I should have done. Yet he is not to be blamed, for he followed his best judgment." Spurgeon was as magnanimous as ever.

Although some regarded the resolution as an instrument of peace, it was regarded by most as a gage of battle—for or against Spurgeon. The Assembly readily understood this, and so voted. The Rev. Henry Oakley, who later also withdrew from the Union on the issue, describes the scene as follows:

I was present at the City Temple when the motion was moved, seconded and carried. Possibly the City Temple was as full as it could be. I was there very early, but found only a "standing seat" in the aisle of the back gallery. I listened to the speeches. The only one of which I have any distinct remembrance was that of Mr. Charles Williams. He quoted Tennyson in favor of a liberal theology and in justification of doubt. The moment of voting came. Only those in the area were qualified to vote as members of the assembly. When the motion of censure was put a forest of hands went up. "Against," called the chairman, Dr. Clifford. I did not see any hands, but history records that there were *seven*. Without any announcement of numbers the vast assembly broke into tumultuous cheering, and cheering and cheering yet. From some of the older men their pent-up hostility found vent; from many of the younger men wild resistance to "any obscurantist trammels," as they said, broke loose. It was a strange scene. I viewed it almost with tears. I stood near a "Spurgeon's man" whom I knew very well. Mr. Spurgeon had welcomed him from a very lowly position. He went almost wild with delight at this censure of his great and generous master. I say it was a strange scene, that that vast assembly should be so outrageously delighted at the condemnation of the greatest, noblest and grandest leader of their faith.

This eye-witness account is very significant. It shows that the resolution was regarded as a condemnation of Spurgeon for raising non-existing issues and making insubstantial charges. The religious press widely reflected this attitude. That a man deeply devoted to the Redeemer, and a faithful advocate of the Evangelical Faith as Spurgeon, one who had led hundreds into salvation, and who had, moreover, raised the Baptist denomination to a position of numerical strength in the country, should have been so censured by the Baptist Union Council, and so condemned by the Baptist Assembly, is a sad and disgraceful thing. Perhaps if Spurgeon could have addressed both Council and Assembly, thought Dr. Fullerton, the outcome might have been different. Probably not. Dr. Booth's concealing tactics, the Union's unwillingness to view the matter in the light of Scripture, and the strong personal hostility to Spurgeon on the part of some, make it unlikely that any further effort on his part would have done any good. Far from "the charges ought never to have been made" attitude, they most certainly should have been made. The cancer of unbelief and of rationalism was already working in the Union. Dr. Booth himself, as we have seen, had already raised the matter before Spurgeon ever made any protest. But the Secretary of the Baptist Union was not willing to have the matter examined too deeply lest a split in the Union result. Once again expediency triumphed over principle. Well might Dr. Carlile sigh, "Spurgeon was never righted."

How did the great preacher react and respond to the vote of censure? In the only way that Mr. Valiant-for-Truth could. In his magazine *The Sword and Trowel* he wrote:

The censure passed upon me by the Council of the Baptist Union will be weighed by the faithful, and estimated at its true value. "Afterwards they have no more that they can do." I brought no charges before members of the Council, because they could only judge by their constitution, and that document lays down no doctrinal basis except the belief that "the immersion of believers is the only Christian baptism." Even the mention of evangelical sentiments has been cut out from their printed program. No one can be heterodox under this constitution, unless he should forswear his baptism. I offered to pay the fee for Counsel's opinion upon this matter, but my offer was not accepted by the deputation. There was, therefore, nothing for me to work upon whatever evidence I might bring. What would be the use of exposing myself to threatened lawsuits to gain nothing at all? Whatever may be said to the contrary, if we go to its authorized declaration of principles, it is clear that the Union is incompetent for any Doctrinal Judgment, except it should be needful to ascertain a person's views on baptism. I decline to submit to it any case which would be quite beyond its powers. Would any rational man do otherwise? I have rather too much proof than too little, but I am not going to involve others in litigation when nothing is to be gained.

I do not complain of the censure of the Council, or feel the least about it. But was this the intent of its loving resolution? Is this the claw that was concealed by the velvet pad of its vote to send four doctors of divinity to me "to deliberate how the unity of the denomination can be maintained in truth, and love, and good works?" Did those who passed that resolution mean—We send these four men to put him the question? Why then did they not say so? Did the world ever hear of such a result of a "deliberation"? The person with whom they deliberate upon union "in truth, and love, and goods works" is questioned and condemned! Let plain-sailing Christian men judge between me and this Council, but let no man imagine that I shall cease from my protests against false doctrine, or lay down the sword of which I have thrown away the scabbard. However much invited to do so, I shall not commence personalities nor disclose the wretched facts in all their details; but with confirmatory evidence perpetually pouring in upon me, and a solemn conviction that the dark conspiracy to overthrow the truth must be dragged to light.

I shall not cease to expose doctrinal declension wherever I see it. With the Baptist Union, as such, I have no hampering connection; but so far as it takes its part in the common departure from the truth, it will have to put up with any strictures, although it has so graciously kicked me under pretext of deliberation....

Now that the offensive personage has been finished off, it will be well to forget him, and go on to the main question. Does the Baptist Union hold the doctrine of the future probation? Many of its members avow it. Members of its high-handed Council glory in it. It could somewhat clear its blurred reputation if it passed a resolution setting forth that it rejected the dream of future probation and restoration as unscriptural, un-Protestant, and a stranger among Baptists. If it does not do so, we may expect to hear a full-blown purgatory preached, and prayers for the dead will follow as a matter of course. Friends are welcome to say what they like about Spurgeon, but what about the Gospel? And what about those who are preaching new doctrines?

The last thing we should care to see would be trials for heresy. These do more harm than good. But there is no need for them. If there be certain definite doctrines laid down, men who honestly differ will go; and if they do not, their remaining will not be the fault of their brethren. The Baptist Union could readily clear itself without going into personal details. Let it tell the world what it believes. And yet we do not know whether its present Council could be trusted to do that; it might say one thing and mean another.

Meanwhile, we look for a gracious revival as the true antidote for the new unbelief. The truth is being preached more boldly already, and we look for corresponding fruit. Prayer goes up to God day and night, and a blessing must come as the result of it. The tender sympathy which we continue to receive from all sections of the Church is a proof that the Lord has thousands of faithful ones still in the land; while the horribly blasphemous letters which are sent to us prove that infidels and men of the world regard our opponents as the advocates of theories with which atheists agree. They look on us as benighted, old-fashioned Puritans, almost beneath their scorn; and we are grateful to them for their unconscious witness to our fidelity.

Thus did Mr. Valiant-for-Truth reply to the censure vote. A trumpet-blast and hammer blows indeed, quite in the manner of good John Bunyan, from whom he had learned so much. One wonders whether, if his opponents read it, they were made to feel ashamed. But Spurgeon had inner, spiritual consolations. He knew that his beloved Master had been attacked and vilified in the self-same way, and he took refuge in Him.

If many of Spurgeon's friends forsook him, others rallied to his support. Evangelicals in many other denominations spoke out and wrote on his side. The Evangelical Alliance was staunch in his support. The Rev. Robert Shindler, who first used the phrase "Down Grade" in his *Sword and Trowel* articles, wrote:

> Never shall we forget the first meeting called by the Alliance for testimony to the fundamental truths of the Gospel, which was held in Exeter Hall. The reception given by the audience to Mr. Spurgeon when he rose to speak was overpowering in its fervor and heartiness. We occupied a seat on the platform near enough to witness the powerful emotions that agitated him, and the tears that streamed down his cheeks as he listened to the previous speakers; and though only a very few of his Baptist brethren were present, there was not wanting such a display of sympathy as must have cheered and comforted his heart.

The question has often been raised as to whether Spurgeon should have founded another denomination, "conservative Evangelical" or fundamentalist. There were many at the time who urged him to do so. Many ministers and churches would have joined him. He even considered it at one time. In the last of the four "Down Grade" articles in *The Sword and Trowel* he expressed the hope that "the day would come when, in a larger communion than any sect can offer, all those who are one in Christ may be able to blend in manifest unity." Undoubtedly Spurgeon could have founded a new body of believers, in church fellowship, on a sound doctrinal basis throughout the country, and it would have been successful and fruitful and enduring. But his strength was gone. He was an ailing man. It was too late. In the next century just such a body was formed, "The Fellowship of Independent Evangelical Churches," with a definitely Scriptural and Evangelical basis of faith. It now numbers more than two hundred and fifty churches, some of which are those that left the Baptist Union with Spurgeon.

A curious echo of the "Down Grade" controversy was heard long after—in 1915. The First World War was in full swing, and many there were who longed for peace—not only amongst the nations, but amongst disunited Christians. At the Baptist Union Assembly in that year a resolution was proposed as follows:

> That without seeking to reinterpret the past, but simply in the interests of spiritual unity and denominational effectiveness, this Assembly thinks that the time has come to delete from its records the Minute of

April 23, 1888, which has reference to C. H. Spurgeon.

One wonders how many were there who were present on the previous occasion when Spurgeon was censured. Dr. John Clifford was there, however, and had no intention of allowing the previous censure to be reversed. He moved as an amendment, that after the introductory clause the motion should run:

> ... this Assembly of the Baptist Union of Great Britain and Ireland declines to reopen the question of the Minute of April 23, 1888, referred to by the mover of the resolution.

It is sad to recall that the amendment was carried by a large majority. So the censure still stands, and the unmerited stain on Mr. Valiant-for-Truth remains. When the Baptist Union built the Baptist Church House in London as the headquarters of their activities, it placed a commanding statue of C. H. Spurgeon in the entrance hall. Many are glad to see it there, but some reflect somewhat sadly that it seems to be a case of "stoning the prophets" and afterwards "building their sepulchres."

What is very clear is that the tide of advanced liberal theology and unscriptural teaching which Spurgeon sought in vain to stem, has swept on steadily and with increased momentum since his day; and few, in any denomination, now hold the doctrines associated with the name of Spurgeon.

We end this re-examination of this famous controversy with the words of an eye-witness already quoted, the Rev. Henry Oakley:

> Many blamed Spurgeon for leaving the Union. They said he should remain to cast out the evil. I remember one such minister—a Doctor of Divinity and a man of standing—who did so. At the last session of the Baptist Union that he ever attended he rose and made an earnest appeal for the brethren to return to the doctrines of grace as their fathers held them, for their own spiritual refreshment and for the salvation of the souls of men. Dr. Newton Marshall, who at that time was one of the bright stars of the Union, wrote in the *Baptist Times:* "It was a pathetic scene, the old man pleading for an order of things that had as surely passed away as the spinning-jenny and the tinderbox. If the pathos of it had not been so deep, the whole scene would have been amusing. The appeal was listened to in silence." The old minister must have read the words, *and learned that Spurgeon was right.* (My italics.)

Chapter 12
Servant of the Lord

God is not otherwise to be enjoyed than as He is obeyed. Nor indeed are the notions of Him as a Lord to be obeyed and as a good to be enjoyed, entirely distinct; but are interwoven and do run into one another. We obey Him even in enjoying Him; it being part of our enjoined duty to set our hearts upon Him as our best and highest good; and we enjoy Him in obeying Him; the advantage and benefit of His government being a real and most momentous part of that good which we enjoy from Him and in Him.

—JOHN HOWE, OF DELIGHTING IN GOD

In 1880 Spurgeon and his family moved to a large house, "Westwood," on Beulah Hill, Upper Norwood. It had been suggested to him some time previously that Mrs. Spurgeon would have better health if they lived on higher ground. Some business affairs took him to Upper Norwood, and walking up Beulah Hill he noticed the house was for sale. When he inspected it he thought that it was too grand. That very day, however, a builder called on him and asked if he would consider selling the house at Clapham as his neighbor wanted it for a son-in-law. This appeared to be providential to Spurgeon, especially when he discovered that he could have "Westwood" for only a little more than his existing house would realize. He thereupon bought "Westwood," almost a palatial residence, with its miniature tower, spacious rooms, wide lawns, rose garden, vinery and conservatory, together with some small fields beyond on which his Susannah grazed two or three cows.

They lived in some style. There was a butler, a cook, maids, gardeners and a coachman. The butler, old George Lovejoy, a faithful servant

Westwood

of many years, was reputed to know his master's sermons almost as well as Sir William Robertson Nicoll of the *British Weekly*, an unrivalled authority. There was also an amanuensis,[45] Mr. J. L. Keys, and a secretary, the Rev. Joseph Harrald, Pastor of Beulah Baptist Chapel, West Norwood, whom Spurgeon called his "Armour-bearer."

Spurgeon kept a carriage, a handsome affair drawn by two splendid coach horses, regarded as the best in London. They were considered better horses even than those belonging to His Grace the Archbishop of Canterbury at Lambeth Palace, who was glad to borrow them on several royal occasions! When some ultra-Sabbatarian objected to Spurgeon working the horses on Sunday, he pleasantly remarked that they were Jews and always rested on Saturdays! Spurgeon drove down from

---

45. An assistant who takes dictation or copies something that is already written; similar to a personal secretary.

the heights of Norwood to the Tabernacle at Southwark twice every Sunday and back again. Perhaps had he walked part of the way he would not have become so stout, but of course it has to be remembered that he suffered much from gout in his feet, and often had to use a stick.

He had a spacious library lined with books, his beloved Puritans nearest to his desk; a smaller inner sanctum adjoining was fitted up for Susannah. He delighted in his gardens, especially the rose garden, and as a countryman he knew the names of most of the flowers and plants. Mrs. Spurgeon was busily occupied with her "book fund," and with the help of a secretary, Miss Thorne, sent out parcels of books to many ministers. She distributed over 200,000 volumes in all, many of them being her husband's own works.

No record of the great preacher's life and labors would be complete without mention of the books he himself wrote or edited. How did he manage to produce so many—135 volumes of which he was the author and twenty-eight which he edited? The answer is that while other ministers spent the week writing sermons, he spent it in writing books or editing magazines. He was a man of unwearied application, and he was never idle. In spite of his constant preaching, traveling, the oversight of a church with 6,000 members, the running of a College and an Orphanage, and many other enterprises, he contrived to make a notable contribution to Evangelical literature, much of which is as fresh and vital today as when he penned it.

His first book, apart from his first volume of sermons, was *The Saint and His Saviour*. It was concerned with "the progress of the soul in the knowledge of Jesus." It has been constantly reprinted, and remains a classic of the spiritual life. He writes of the despised Friend, Jesus desired, Jesus pardoning, Joy at conversion, the Believer complete in Christ, love to Jesus, Jesus in the hour of trouble, etc. A book as Christo-centric as its author, and a blessing to multitudes.

Another early work was *John Plowman's Talk*, and its sequel *John Plowman's Pictures*, little books of proverbial philosophy for plain people, written in a pungent, witty manner. They were tremendously popular in their day, and Dr. Stalker thought that the first, at any rate, "is certain of immortality among the popular classics of England." But, alas, tastes in classics change; it has disappeared into that realm from which many best-sellers never reappear!

The greatest of his works was *The Treasury of David*, a seven volume commentary on the Psalms. Not only are there expositions of every verse, but also extracts from authors of all ages. It shows vast reading and deeply spiritual meditation. Dr. J. H. Jowett, no mean judge, said of it: "I have for many years sought and found nutriment for my own pulpit in this marvelous exposition. He is not eclipsed even when set in the radiant succession of Calvin and Luther and Paul." The first volume was published in 1869, and the last in 1885. For twenty years he toiled at it in his spare time, and it is true to say that no work of his, apart from his Sermons, has so enriched the spiritual life of all branches of the Church. Into these volumes he put his very heart, his experience, his inmost soul. *The Treasury of David* has been constantly reprinted in England and in America, and will remain as an authority on the Psalms while the earth remains.

Spurgeon also wrote a commentary on Matthew's Gospel entitled *The Gospel of the Kingdom,* full of original observations, shrewd comments, and much exalting of Christ. It does not deserve to be forgotten. *All of Grace,* a little book intended for those seeking Christ, is a straightforward account of the plan of salvation, full of loving exhortation and wise counsel. A companion volume to this is *According to Promise,* intended to build up the young believer in the faith.

The two volumes of *Lectures to My Students* and *Commenting and Commentaries* have already been mentioned; but one would like to draw particular attention to the first lecture in the second volume, "The Holy Spirit in Connection with our Ministry," as being full of light and power, and one which every minister might well ponder prayerfully once a year.

Spurgeon prepared three volumes of daily readings: *Morning by Morning, Evening by Evening* and *The Cheque-book of the Bank of Faith.* These are spiritual treasure-chests of rich and rare things, and will remain a refreshment of soul and a guide of life to all who use them. He also published two books of sermon illustrations and anecdotes—*Feathers for Arrows* and *The Salt Cellars.*

In addition to the sixty-three volumes of sermons, many other books of sermons on kindred themes such as The Parables, The Miracles, Farm Sermons, Messages for the Multitudes were also issued. Nor must it be forgotten that for twenty-eight years he was the editor of the magazine *The Sword and the Trowel,* commenced in 1865. It had as its subtitle "A Record of Combat with Sin, and Labour for the Lord." To this he contributed many articles of permanent spiritual value, and by means of it rallied his friends and well-wishers in the service of the Gospel, and the progress of the causes he had at heart. By means of it, also, a great deal of the money required for the Tabernacle, College, and Orphanage was raised.

The ultimate fate of his library makes sad reading. Some of the 12,000 volumes were given to the Pastors' College library and to friends, but the bulk of the 7,000 or more priceless collection of Puritan works was allowed to be sold to America, without any effort by Spurgeon-lovers to retain it for Britain! With the help of a Baptist editor, Dr. J. W. Thirtle, it was sold in 1905 for as little as £500 to the William Jewell College, Missouri. They certainly had a bargain! There they are in a remote American college, undivided and unknown, a collection of Puritan books unrivaled in the world, and beyond price. There are also the Bibles he used at New Park Street and at "Westwood." However, one comforting thought comes to mind regarding this melancholy business. In the providence of God, as John Flavel would say, events may have been "wheeled about," so that the whole collection of volumes may have been saved from the Nazi blitz on London, when millions of books were blasted to nothing in the environs of St. Paul Cathedral one bitter night in the Second World War. But still, Missouri is a long way to go to consult the books which Spurgeon handled, and which made him "heir of the Puritans."

Sincerity was a foremost characteristic of all his writings. It is as though he says to us: "Reader, do you mean business with God? What does your life look like in the searching light of Eternity? Are you saved and rejoicing in the grace and goodness of the Lord? Nothing matters but your being made right with God by the sacrifice of His Son." His main purpose was the salvation of men's souls.

Some have said that Spurgeon was the last of the Puritans, but this is a great mistake. He stirred up tens of thousands to read the Puritans for themselves, and to fashion life according to their principles. And today they are being studied and followed as never before.

What shall we say of the inner life of C. H. Spurgeon? How impossible to do more than hint at some of its great qualities. He was a man of faith and hope and love and prayer. He once observed that although he found it difficult to remain on his knees for half an hour, yet he was often in prayer in the midst of his duties, or walking along a road.

The habit of prayer is good, but the spirit of prayer is better. Regular retirement is to be maintained, but continued communion with God is to be our aim. As a rule, we ministers ought never to be many minutes without actually lifting up our hearts in prayer. Some of us could honestly say that we are seldom a quarter of an hour without speaking to God, and that not as a duty, but as an instinct, a habit of the new nature.

He knew the meaning of Paul's exhortation, "Pray without ceasing." "I always feel it well," he said, "to put a few words of prayer between everything I do." One of his students records how once, in a railway carriage, they knelt down and spent a time in prayer. He never wrote a letter without raising his heart to God for guidance.

Dr. Wayland Hoyte says:

I was walking with him in some woods one day, and as we strolled under the shadow of the summer foliage we came upon a log lying athwart the path. "Come," said he, as naturally as one would say it if he were hungry and bread were put before him, "come, let us pray." And kneeling beside the log, he lifted his soul to God in the most loving outpouring and yet reverent prayer. Then rising from his knees as naturally, he went strolling on, talking about this and that. The prayer was no parenthesis interjected. It was something that belonged as much to the habit of his mind as breathing did to the habit of his body.

Dr. Theodore Cuyler records a similar happening. In one of the Surrey woods they were walking and talking in high spirits, when suddenly Spurgeon stopped and said: "Come, Theodore, let us thank God for laughter." And they did. He told Dr. W. Y. Fullerton that he never got so near God as on the Tabernacle platform when he prayed. He said to his students in one of his Friday afternoon lectures:

Sometimes you will enjoy closer fellowship with God in prayer in the pulpit than you have known anywhere else. To me, my greatest secrecy in prayer has often been in public; my truest loneliness with God has occurred to me while pleading in the midst of thousands. I have opened my eyes at the close of a prayer and come back to the assembly with a sort of a shock at finding myself upon earth and among men.

The sense of blessedness in prayer on such occasions was doubtless helped by the fact that he was ministering amongst a praying people. They upheld their Pastor greatly at the Throne of Grace, and the atmosphere at the Tabernacle, as we have already seen, was often deeply charged with spiritual power. He was borne up on the wings of the

prayers of others, as well as by his own devotional frame of mind.
The Rev. W. W. Williams said:

> It was marvelous to hear his soliloquies at the Lord's Table—his lan-
> guage there would have been considered extravagant if one did not
> know how perfectly real it was. From praying he would take to talking,
> and from talking he would stand and soliloquize about his Lord, and
> the audience felt that he was simply enraptured with Him.

The best of men are but men at the best, and Spurgeon also more
than once knew what it was to be in the clutches of Giant Despair. After
the terrible tragedy at the Surrey Music Hall he was deeply depressed,
as we have seen, but the Word of God came in power to refresh his soul.
Once, on holiday in the country, and feeling gloomy and dispirited, he
went to a little Methodist Chapel one Sunday morning where the service was conducted by a local preacher. He tells us that while he listened:

> The tears flowed from my eyes—I was moved to the deepest emotion
> by every sentence of the sermon, and I felt all my difficulties removed,
> for the Gospel, I saw, was very dear to me, and had a wonderful effect
> on my heart. I went to the preacher and said, "I thank you very much
> for the sermon." He asked who I was, and when I told him he turned
> as red as possible, and said, "Why, it was one of your own sermons I
> preached this morning." "Yes," I said, "I know it was; but that was the
> very message I wanted to hear, because I then saw that I did enjoy the
> very word I myself preached."

Many are the stories told of his preaching. He relates several himself
in his first book of *Lectures to my Students*.

> When I lived at Cambridge I had, as usual, to preach in the evening at
> a neighboring village, to which I had to walk. After reading and medi-
> tating all day, I could not meet with the right text. I prayed, I medi-
> tated, I turned from one verse to another, but the mind would not take
> hold, or I was as John Bunyan would say, "much tumbled up and
> down in my thoughts." Just then I walked to the window and looked
> out. On the other side of the narrow street in which I lived I saw a
> poor, solitary canary upon the slates, surrounded by a crowd of spar-
> rows, who were all tearing at it as though they would tear it to pieces.
> At that moment the verse came to my mind, "Mine heritage is unto
> me as a speckled bird, the birds round about are against her." I walked
> off in the greatest possible composure, considered the passage during
> my long and lonely walk, and preached upon the peculiar people, and

the persecutions of their enemies, with freedom and ease to myself, and I believe with comfort to my rustic audience.

Once at New Park Street Chapel he had an extraordinary experience.

I had passed happily through all the early parts of divine service in the evening of the Sabbath, and was giving out the hymn before sermon. I opened the Bible to find the text, which I had carefully studied as the topic of discourse, when on the opposite page another passage of Scripture sprang upon me like a lion from the thicket, with vastly more power than I had felt when considering the text which I had chosen. The people were singing and I was singing. I was at an impasse between two, and my mind hung as in the balances. I was naturally desirous to run in the track which I had carefully planned, but the other text would take no refusal. At last I thought within myself: "Well, I would like to preach the sermon which I have prepared, and it is a great risk to run to strike out a new line of thought, but still as this text constrains me, it may be of the Lord, and therefore I will venture upon it, come what may."

I passed through the first head with considerable liberty, speaking perfectly extemporaneously both as to thought and word. The second point was dwelt upon with a consciousness of unusual quiet efficient power, but I had no idea what the third would or could be, for the text yielded no matter just then, nor can I tell even now what I could have done had not an event occurred upon which I had never calculated.... In one moment we were in total darkness—the gas had gone out, and as the aisles were choked with people, and the place everywhere crowded, it was a great peril, but a great blessing. What was I to do then? The people were a little frightened, but I quieted them instantly by telling them not to be at all alarmed, though the gas was out, for it would soon be relit; and as for myself, having no manuscript, I could speak just as well in the dark as in the light, if they would be so good as to sit and listen. I turned at once to the well-known text which speaks of the child of light walking in darkness, and the child of darkness walking in the light, and found appropriate remarks and illustrations pouring in upon me; and when the lamps were relit I saw before me an audience as rapt and subdued as ever a man beheld in his life. The odd thing of all was that some few church meetings afterwards, two persons came forward to make confession of their faith, who professed to have been converted that evening; the first owed her conversion to the former part of the discourse, which was on the new text that came to me, and the other traced his awakening to the latter part, which was occasioned by the sudden darkness. Thus, you see, Providence befriended me. I cast myself upon God, and His arrangements quenched the light at the proper time for me. Some may ridicule, but I adore; others may even censure, but I rejoice.

C. H. Spurgeon was once announced to preach at Haverhill in Suffolk, and unavoidably was late in arriving. So his grandfather, the Rev. James Spurgeon of Stambourne, began the service, and as his grandson was still absent he proceeded with the sermon, choosing as his text, "By grace ye are saved." He had proceeded for a few minutes when some unrest at the door made him aware that his famous grandson had arrived. "Here comes my grandson," the old man exclaimed. "He can preach the Gospel better than I can, but you cannot preach a better Gospel, can you, Charles?" Walking up the aisle towards the pulpit his grandson replied, "You can preach better than I can, pray go on." His grandfather refused, but he told him the text, explaining that he had already shown the people the source and fountain-head of salvation— "grace," and was now speaking of the channel of it—"through faith." Charles Spurgeon took up the theme, and advanced to the next point—"but not of yourselves"—and was setting forth the weakness and inability of human nature to effect salvation, when his grandfather interrupted and said, "I know most about that." So for five minutes he discoursed, and then his grandson continued again, having his grandfather's whispered commendation, "Good, good!" as he warmed to his subject, until at some special point the old man called out, "Tell them that again, Charles." Ever after, when Charles recalled the text, there came to him with great intensity the words of the old minister: "Tell them that again, Charles."

He preached also for his father who was minister of the Congregational Church at Cross Street, Islington. The white-haired old man shared the pulpit with his renowned son, very proud of such a notable occasion. Charles referred to their absolute union of heart and opinion except upon one point. "My dear father, here, and I agree admirably," he told the congregation, "the only difference we have is that there is a little water between us!"

In the Surrey Gardens Music Hall one morning several men kept hats on even after the service had begun. After the first hymn Spurgeon told the congregation that he had recently visited a Jewish synagogue, and in accordance with the custom of the place he had worn his hat during the service. "But," he said, "it is the Christian practice to uncover in a place of worship. I will therefore ask these young, Jewish gentlemen kindly to remove their hats." And they did.

On many occasions he felt guided to say some unusual thing which went home to hearts in the congregation. He once said that there was a man sitting in the gallery with a bottle of gin in his pocket. In fact there was such a man, and he was startled into conversion. One Sunday evening Spurgeon pointed to the gallery and said, "Young man, the gloves in your pocket are not paid for." After the service a young man came to the vestry beseeching the preacher not to say anything more about it, and he also was brought under conviction of sin and was led to Christ. On another occasion a woman who had determined on suicide came in with the crowd to hear a last message that might prepare her to die. The text was "Seest thou this woman...?" It was a message that prepared her to live, for divine grace changed her heart that night. On yet another occasion, Spurgeon pointed to the gallery and said, "There is a man sitting there who is a shoemaker; he keeps his shop open on Sundays; it was open last Sabbath morning. He took ninepence, and there was fourpence profit on it: his soul is sold to Satan for fourpence!" There actually was a shoemaker sitting there, who had acted exactly as Spurgeon had described, although the preacher knew nothing of him. The vivid shot at a venture pierced the joints of his armor, and he was converted.

In *The Sword and Trowel* Spurgeon related how he called at City Road Chapel, the London headquarters of Methodism, in August 1880, while the Wesleyan Conference was in full session. He had been very ill, and had no intention of speaking to the Methodist brethren but went to see the manager of the refreshment department in order to see how their meal arrangements were carried through, in view of the fact that the Baptist Union meetings were soon to be held. He intended to steal in and out quietly, but he was recognized, of course, and before he knew what was happening he had been conducted on to the platform, and was being introduced to the Assembly by Dr. Morley Punshon. He was received with great affection and invited to address the brethren. He was quite unprepared, but looked to God for help, and was given a timely and uplifting message for the Conference. It was received with enthusiasm. This was a truly remarkable incident, for the Methodists well knew that on certain points of doctrine he was totally opposed to them, and did not mind saying so. But they knew, and Spurgeon knew also, that they were united in the essential doctrines of salvation through faith in the blood of Jesus and regeneration by the Holy Spirit. He liked to remember this as a spontaneous outburst of brotherly love in Christ, a unity which had a solid foundation.

Spurgeon discovered that the widow of Christmas Evans, the great Welsh preacher, was living in deep poverty, and arranged for a pension to be paid for her for the rest of her life. Many were the appeals for financial help made to him, from individuals and from good causes, and as far as he was able he generally contributed.

D. L. Moody, the famous American evangelist, and Spurgeon had a great regard and admiration for one another. He preached in the Tabernacle several times, and induced Spurgeon to preach for him during his Evangelical campaign in London. He once wrote to Spurgeon, "In regard to coming to your Tabernacle, I consider it a great honor to be invited; and, in fact, I should consider it an honor to black your boots...."

When Spurgeon first came to London the greatest preacher in the metropolis was Thomas Binney, author of the hymn, "Eternal Light, Eternal Light," and a leading Nonconformist of his day. At first he was inclined to deride the boy in the pulpit as a charlatan, but he quickly saw his mistake, and publicly said, "I have enjoyed some amount of popularity; I have always been able to draw together a congregation; but in the person of Mr. Spurgeon we see a young man, be he who he may, and come whence he will, who at twenty-four hours' notice can command a congregation of 20,000 people. Now I have never been able to do that, and I never knew of anybody else who could do it."

Even when he was in poor health, Spurgeon was never off duty for the Lord. Preaching at the Metropolitan Tabernacle on September 28, 1862, he said:

When I was sore sick some three years or more ago, I walked about to recover strength, and walking through the town of Wandsworth, I thought, "How few attend a place of worship here. Here are various churches, but there is ample room for one of our own faith and order, something must be done." I thought, "If I could start a man here preaching the Word what good might be done." The next day, some four friends from the town called to see me, one a Baptist, and the three others were desirous of baptism: "Would I come there and form a church?" We took the large rooms at a tavern, and preaching has been carried on there ever since. Beginning with four, the church has

Wandsworth

increased to one-hundred-and-fifty. I have aided the interest by going there continually and preaching and helping to support the minister. Now, a beautiful piece of ground has been taken, and a chapel is to be erected, and I firmly believe there will be a very strong cause raised.

And he concluded with a plea for a good collection for this new work.

Spurgeon was a founder member of the London Baptist Association, and stirred up his fellow Baptists to plant and nurture new churches in rapidly growing London. Many churches were thus built, his aim being at least one new church every year. Many of the foundation stones of Baptist churches in the Greater London area were laid by C. H. Spurgeon. None have done more than he to increase the Baptist denomination in London and the southern counties.

Driving home in a cab one night, he got into conversation with the cab-driver. "It is a long time since I drove you last, sir," said he. "Did you ever drive me before?" asked Spurgeon. "I do not recollect you." "Oh yes," said the man, "it is about fourteen years ago, but if you have forgotten me, perhaps you will remember this," and pulled a New Testament out of his pocket. "What," said the preacher, "did I give you that?" "Yes, sir, and you spoke to me about my soul, and nobody had ever done that before. I have never forgotten it." "And haven't you worn the Testament out in all these years?" "No, sir. I wouldn't let it be worn out.

I have had it new bound."

One Sunday night a burglar broke into "Westwood" and stole a few small articles, including a gold-headed stick with Spurgeon's name engraved on it. By means of the stick the intruder was discovered and arrested when he tried to dispose of it. The burglar thereupon wrote to Spurgeon saying that he did not know that it was "the horflings'[46] Spurgeon" who lived there, and ended by saying, "Why don't you shut your windows and keep a dog?" Spurgeon took the burglar's advice, and bought a bulldog named "Punch" who gave his master much pleasure.

News of the robbery led the journal *Punch* to include an article entitled, "Diary of a Burglar." Various "jobs" in his profession are mentioned, and then:

> ˙ast night I did a stylish little piece of work. Robbed Spurgeon's house. ᴧ ˒t so much for the [loot] as to create a sensation. Have always been a follower and admirer of his, but shouldn't have been if I'd known how precious few valuables he keeps in the establishment. Nothing but tracts and reports, and "Notes for discourses." ... Shall really think of giving up my pew—quite disgusted.

Another burglar story is connected with the Tabernacle. In 1890 the clock on the preacher's rostrum was stolen by a burglar, who left a note saying that "the reverend gentleman was less concerned with Time than with Eternity" so would never miss the clock!

Spurgeon once had an encounter with a dangerous madman who came to the Tabernacle vestry, shut the door, and declared that he had come to cut Spurgeon's throat. Spurgeon regarded him coolly. "I would not do that," he said, "see what a mess it would make on the carpet." "Oh, I had never thought of that," said the madman, and was quietly led away.

And once Spurgeon came face to face with a murderer. One day a young man called on him at "Westwood" and represented himself as the son of the famous American preacher, Henry Ward Beecher. Spurgeon took him round his garden while they talked. He brought, he said, his father's esteem and affection, and told many stories, mostly fictitious, about Beecher's family and church. When Spurgeon presently

---

46. This word is the transliteration of a term used by the burglar in his own dialect; it carries the idea of the "honorable" or "respectable" Mr. Spurgeon.

said he must bid him goodbye, the young man asked if he would oblige him by cashing a check. Spurgeon's suspicions were instantly aroused, and he refused. The young man quickly left him. A few days afterwards a man was robbed and murdered in a tunnel on the Brighton railway. A young man named Lefroy was arrested, tried, condemned, and executed for the murder, and when his portrait appeared in the newspapers Spurgeon recognized his visitor.

It was a very happy and peaceful life at "Westwood," although both Charles and Susannah were frequently burdened with physical sufferings. The twin sons, Charles and Thomas, were a great delight to them in their growing years. It gave them deep joy when they were baptized by their father at the Metropolitan Tabernacle, and later on began to preach in a cottage at Wandsworth. Both started out in business careers, Charles in a city merchant's office, Thomas as a wood engraver. But their preaching abilities were outstanding, and both entered the ministry. Charles held much blessed pastorates at Greenwich, Nottingham, Cheltenham and Hove, and eventually became his father's successor at the Orphanage. Thomas went out to Australia, and there, and also in New Zealand, exercised faithful ministries, before returning home to become successor to his great father at the Metropolitan Tabernacle. There he labored until his death in 1917.

Spurgeon resolutely refused to be ordained, although his deacons urged it upon him. He did not think that man could convey any spiritual grace or blessing upon him that God had not already given. Nor would he wear any distinctive clerical dress or collar, regarding such things as priestly trappings. At the beginning of his ministry he used the courtesy title Reverend, but later dropped this in favor of the word Pastor.

His habit of smoking exposed Spurgeon to much adverse criticism, even by his friends. He smoked heavily throughout his life, and this most probably had a bad effect upon his health. Once he became the center of controversy regarding smoking. An American preacher, Dr. G. F. Pentecost, preached at the Tabernacle on one occasion, dividing the sermon with Spurgeon. All unwittingly, Dr. Pentecost mentioned his struggles in renouncing his cigar, and Spurgeon, when his turn came to speak, most unfortunately declared that he hoped that very evening to smoke a cigar to the glory of God. The press seized joyfully on this incident, and the statement was widely discussed. Could one really smoke to the glory of God? Spurgeon's photograph even appeared on tobacco packets. He wrote a letter to *The Daily Telegraph* in which he acknowledged his smoking habits, but maintained that it was no sin. He claimed liberty so to indulge. He said that smoking relieved his pain, soothed his brain, and helped him to sleep. It was not a very satisfactory letter, and it did not mend matters. No doubt had Spurgeon lived in our own day when medical science has established a connection between smoking and lung cancer, Spurgeon would have thought and acted differently.

Something may here be said about Spurgeon's appearance. When he came to London as a clean-shaven youth, he was slender, and only five-foot-six in height. He had rosy cheeks and a countrified appearance. But he soon put on weight and became the stout, heavy-looking figure

so often seen in the photographs of the time. He never took enough exercise. At about the age of thirty-five he grew a Vandyke[47] beard, and his facial appearance was much improved. (Many of the Puritans wore such beards; was this a coincidence?) He had striking eyes, hazel brown, narrow-lidded, and penetrating in look. He suffered terribly from gout, inherited from his father; his hands were so puffy that, when shaking hands with him, one's fingers sank into his flesh. At one time he became a vegetarian, and in one year, 1887, diminished eight inches in girth. But he resumed meat eating after a few years. His voice, clear as a silver bell, was a marvelous organ for his preaching, and carried to the furthest corner of the great church he built. He had a radiant smile which lit up and transformed his whole face. Truly was it said of him that he was a plain man made beautiful by the grace of God.

Spurgeon wrote a number of hymns—Puritan doctrine set to music! Most have been forgotten, but a number are still deservedly to be found in some hymnbooks, and will be sung as long as believers delight to sing the praises of the Lord with words that express Scriptural truth. We give two of them which reveal the feelings of his heart and the delight of his soul.

A MORNING HYMN

Sweetly the holy hymn
Breaks on the morning air;
Before the world with smoke is dim
We meet to offer prayer.

While flowers are wet with dew,
Dew of our souls, descend;
Ere yet the sun the day renew,
O Lord, Thy Spirit send.

Upon the battlefield,
Before the fight begins,
We seek, O Lord, Thy sheltering shield,
To guard us from our sins.

Ere yet our vessel sails

---

47. A closely trimmed, pointed beard.

Upon the stream of day,
We plead, O Lord, for heavenly gales
To speed us on our way.

On the lone mountain side,
Before the morning's light,
The Man of sorrows wept and cried,
And rose refreshed with might.

O hear us, then, for we
Are very weak and frail;
We make the Saviour's name our plea,
And surely must prevail.

A Communion Hymn

Amidst us our Beloved stands,
And bids us view His pierced hands,
Points to His wounded feet and side,
Blest emblems of the Crucified.

What food luxurious loads the board,
When at His table sits the Lord!
The wine how rich, the bread how sweet,
When Jesus deigns[48] the guests to meet!

If now, with eyes defiled and dim,
We see the signs, but see not Him,
O may His love the scales displace,
And bid us see Him face to face!

Thou glorious Bridegroom of our hearts,
Thy present smile a heaven imparts;
O lift the veil, if veil there be,
Let every saint Thy beauties see!

---

48. To think fit or in accordance with one's dignity, or to condescend.

Chapter 13
To Immanuel's Land

If it be pleasant to behold the sun, how blessed a sight will it be to see Christ, the Sun of Righteousness, clothed with our human nature, shining in glory above the angels! Through Christ's flesh, as through a transparent glass, some bright rays and beams of the Godhead shall display themselves to glorified eyes. The sight of God through Christ will be very delightful; His majesty will be mixed with beauty, and sweetened with clemency. "We shall be like Him." The saints shall so see God, as that sight shall transform them into His likeness.

—THOMAS WATSON, *A BODY OF DIVINITY*

The very last occasion on which Charles Haddon Spurgeon preached in the Metropolitan Tabernacle was on Sunday morning, June 7, 1891. He appeared a broken man, prematurely old, although only fifty-seven, his hair white, the lines of anguish on his face. He was so enfeebled that he had to hold on to the back of a chair as he conducted the service. He preached on the text—1 Samuel 30:24, "The Statute of David for Sharing the Spoil." Many, seeing him, must have realized that the end of his ministry was near. His final words in his pulpit, as we have seen, were of "Christ, the most magnanimous of Captains." Faithful unto the last!

The next day, in spite of his weakness, he insisted on going to Stambourne, where he limped about with a photographer who took pictures of his boyhood scenes in preparation for a book of memoirs he was writing. On his return to London he became gravely ill, and for more than a month lay in bed, much of the time unconscious. Mr. W.

E. Gladstone sent a message of sympathy and admiration.

> *Dear Madam,*
>
> *In my own house, darkened at the present time, I have read with sad interest the daily accounts of Mr. Spurgeon's illness; and I cannot help conveying to you the earnest assurance of my sympathy with you and with him, and of my cordial admiration, not only for his splendid powers, but still more of his devoted and unfailing character. May I humbly commend you and him, in all contingencies, to the infinite stores of the Divine love and mercy, and subscribe myself,*
>
> *My dear Madam,*
> *Faithfully yours,*
> *W. E. Gladstone.*

When Mrs. Spurgeon wrote a reply, Spurgeon was a little better, and insisted on adding a postscript:

> *P.S. Yours is a word of love such as those only write who have been into the King's Country, and seen much of His face. My heart's love to you.*
>
> *C. H. Spurgeon.*

In August he was sufficiently recovered to send a letter to be read to the Tabernacle congregation:

> *The Lord's Name be praised for first giving and then hearing the loving prayers of His people! Through these prayers my life is prolonged. I feel greatly humbled, and very grateful, at being the object of so great a love and so wonderful an outburst of prayer.*
>
> *I have not strength to say more. Let the Name of the Lord be glorified.*
>
> *Yours most heartily,*
> *C. H. Spurgeon.*

Dr. A. T. Pierson, the much loved American Presbyterian preacher and missionary statesman, was occupying his pulpit for the time being with much acceptance. In October, a fortnight at Eastbourne proved beneficial to the sick man. Then on October 26th, accompanied by Mrs. Spurgeon, Dr. and Mrs. James Spurgeon, and his faithful "Armour-bearer" the Rev. J. W. Harrald, he journeyed to his beloved Mentone in the South of France. It was the first journey Susannah had taken with him for years, but the doctor said that she was well enough to go. It was a dear delight to them to be together at Mentone, and to spend three months of perfect happiness before his Home calling.

Spurgeon had paid nearly twenty annual visits to the place, had seen it grow from a village to a town, and knew well its long tradition. The waters of the Mediterranean were a deep blue, the Alpine mountains that reach down nearly to the shore were beautiful in their soft pastel shades, the olive groves were bright with silver and green, and the sun shone down warm and cheering. Here, if anywhere, he would get better.

For a while he seemed to improve in health and strength. On the last evening of 1891, and on January 1, 1892, he gave two brief addresses at the Hotel Beau-Rivage. He wrote to his son in New Zealand. He wrote a little message to the Head Boy and Head Girl of the Orphanage, sending each a text. On Sunday evenings January 10th and 17th he conducted a brief service in his room, reading some of his own writings. The service on January 17th was the last he ever attended, and at the close the hymn "The Sands of Time Are Sinking" was sung. It was the end of all service on earth for him.

> *The King there, in His beauty,*
> *Without a veil is seen;*
> *It were a well-spent journey,*
> *Though seven deaths lay between:*
> *The Lamb, with His fair army,*
> *Doth on Mount Zion stand,*
> *And glory, glory, dwelleth,*
> *In Immanuel's land.*
>
> *O Christ, He is the fountain,*
> *The deep, sweet well of love;*
> *The streams on earth I've tasted,*

Mentone

More deep I'll drink above:
There, to an ocean fulness,
  His mercy doth expand,
And glory, glory dwelleth
  In Immanuel's land.

I've wrestled on towards heaven,
  'Gainst storm and wind and tide;
Now, like a weary traveller
  That leaneth on his guide,
Amid the shades of evening,
  While sinks life's lingering sand,
I hail the glory dawning
  From Immanuel's land.

On January 20th serious symptoms appeared, and he retired to a bed from which he never rose again. On the 23rd he said to Mr. Harrald, "My work is done." When the end drew near, he whispered,

"Susie." She bent close to listen, clasped his hand in hers and said, "Yes, dear Tirshatha?" And he murmured—the last words before he saw Him face to face—"Oh, wifie, I have had such a blessed time with my Lord!"

On January 27th he became totally unconscious, and remained so until five minutes past eleven on Sunday night, January 31, 1892, when, like his namesake Mr. Valiant-for-Truth, he passed over, and all the trumpets sounded for him on the other side. Mrs. Spurgeon led the little group of relatives and friends by the bedside in prayer and praise.

Years before he had spoken of death:

The dying saint is not in a flurry; he keeps to his old pace—he walks. The last days of a Christian are the most peaceful of his whole career; many a saint has reaped more joy and knowledge when he came to die than ever he knew while he lived. When there is a shadow there must be a light somewhere. The light of Jesus shining upon death throws a shadow across our path; let us therefore rejoice for the Light beyond!

Spurgeon was fifty-seven when he died, worn out with a multitude of labors for the Lord he loved. Strangely enough, many other great saints of God have been ushered into the presence of the King at exactly the same age—John Calvin, William Tyndale, Jonathan Edwards, Jeremy Taylor, and George Whitefield.

On February 4th a Memorial Service was held at the Presbyterian Church, Mentone, conducted by the Rev. J. E. Somerville, and then the coffin was brought home to England. The news of his home-call flashed round the world, and the newspapers contained long articles concerning his life and ministry.

At the Metropolitan Tabernacle, the congregation held a fitting memorial to his great labors. Surgeon's body lay in state, and no less than 60,000 persons filed past the coffin to pay their tribute to the Prince of Preachers. On the coffin lay a Bible, open at the text which led to his conversion, "Look unto Me, and be ye saved, all the ends of the earth." A day or so later, four successive Memorial Services were held in the great church where his beautiful voice would never be heard again. In large letters over his pulpit was inscribed the text he had last quoted, "I have fought a good fight, I have finished my course, I have kept the faith," 2 Timothy 4:7. Moving tributes were paid to the dead champion by Dr. A. T. Pierson, Dr. James Spurgeon, Rev. Archibald Brown, and Rev. Joseph Harrald, while Ira D. Sankey, of the famous Moody and

The funeral procession

Sankey evangelistic team, sang Gospel solos. Deeply moving, indeed, were these services, filled not only with honor for the dead saint, but also of praise for the living Lord.

Spurgeon had expressed a wish to be buried in the grounds of the Stockwell Orphanage, but owing to the proximity of the underground railway, this proved impracticable. His body was therefore laid to rest in the West Norwood Cemetery. Great crowds lined the streets as the forty carriages of the funeral procession went by, almost all were dressed in black. At the gates of the Orphanage the children, dressed in black, sat on a raised platform, and sang in their childish voices:

> *The Homeland, the Homeland,*
> *The land of the Free-born;*
> *There's no night in the Homeland,*
> *But aye the fadeless morn.*

At the grave a deeply impressive service took place, conducted by Dr. A. T. Pierson. Archibald Brown of East London Tabernacle, one of Spurgeon's closest and staunchest friends, pronounced a touching eulogy:

Beloved President, Faithful Pastor, Prince of Preachers, Brother Beloved, Dear Spurgeon—we bid thee not "Farewell," but only for a little while "Good-night." You shall rise soon at the first dawn of the Resurrection-day of the redeemed. Yet is the good-night not ours to bid but yours; it is we who linger in the darkness; thou art in God's holy light. Our night shall soon be passed and with it all our weeping. Then with yours, our songs shall greet the morning of the day that knows no cloud nor close; for there is not night there.

Hard worker in the field! thy toil is ended. Straight has been the furrow thou hast ploughed. No looking back has marred thy course. Harvests have followed thy patient sowing, and heaven is already rich with your ingathered sheaves, and shall still be enriched through the years yet lying in eternity.

Champion of God! your battle, long and nobly fought is over; your sword which clung to your hand, has dropped at last; a palm branch takes its place. No longer does the helmet press your brow, often weary by its surging thoughts of battle; a victor's wreath from the great Commander's hand has already proved your full reward.

Here, for a little while, shall rest thy precious dust. Then shall thy Well-Beloved come; and at His voice thou shalt spring from thy couch of earth, fashioned like unto His body, into glory. Then spirit, soul and body shall magnify the Lord's redemption. Until then, beloved, sleep. We praise God for thee, and by the blood of the everlasting covenant, hope and expect to praise God with thee. Amen.

Surely no tribute more fitting or more comprehensive could have been uttered. The Bishop of Rochester pronounced the Benediction, and then his friends turned away to take up the battle where he had laid it down.

On his tomb were engraved some lines very dear to Spurgeon:

> *E'er since by faith I saw the stream*
> *Thy flowing wounds supply,*
> *Redeeming love has been my theme*
> *And shall be till I die."*

Very characteristically, some years previously in one of his sermons, Spurgeon attempted to picture the scene at his funeral:

In a little while there will be a concourse of persons in the streets. Methinks I hear someone inquiring:

"What are all these people waiting for?"

"Do you not know? He is to be buried today."

"And who is that?

"It is Spurgeon."

"What—the man that preached at the Tabernacle?"

"Yes, he is to be buried today."

That will happen very soon. And when you see my coffin carried to the silent grave, I should like every one of you, whether converted or not, to be constrained to say, "He did earnestly urge us, in plain and simple language, not to put off the consideration of eternal things; he did entreat us to look to Christ. Now he is gone, our blood is not at his door if we perish."

Mrs. Spurgeon wrote about this time, "For me it is absolutely necessary that I should keep looking up. "He is not here; He is risen," is as true of my beloved as of my beloved Lord. Today he has been a week in Heaven. Oh, the bliss and rapture of seeing his Savior's face! Oh, the welcome home which awaited him as he left this sad earth! Not for a moment do I wish him back, though he was dearer to me than tongue can tell." She continued to reside at "Westwood," busy with her book fund and other good works for the Lord and His people, until her death on October 22, 1903.—She is buried in the same grave as her husband.

> *With mercy and with judgment,*
> *My web of time He wove;*
> *And aye the dews of sorrow*
> *Were lustered with His love;*
> *I'll bless the Hand that guided,*
> *I'll bless the Heart that planned,*
> *When throned where glory dwelleth*
> *In Immanuel's land.*

Chapter 14
"He Being Dead, Yet Speaketh"

Beloved, there is scarce any truth necessary to salvation but you have heard of it once and again from some or other of God's messengers that have been sent to you. You have heard what God is, and how He will be worshipped, even in spirit and in truth, and not according to the inventions and traditions of men. You have heard the doctrine of God's decrees, and of His works of creation and providence opened and applied. You have heard of the sinful and miserable condition of a man in a natural condition. You have heard the doctrine of the covenant of grace, and of the means of our recovery by Christ alone. You have heard Christ set before you in His person, natures, offices, obedience, and sufferings. Oh, labor to remember these. Keep them by you as a choice treasure. Lay them up in your heads and hearts. Let the Word of God, even that Word of His which we have spoken to you in His name, abide with you for ever.

—JOHN WHITLOCK, *FAREWELL SERMONS*

We do well to ponder this appeal from John Whitlock, one of the noble band of men from Emmanuel College, Cambridge, a powerful Puritan minister in Nottingham, and a friend and colleague of Dr. Reynolds. The above passage occurs in his sermon, "Remember, hold fast, and repent" (Rev. 3:3), preached at the time of the Great Ejection of

Nonconformists from the Church of England, on St. Bartholomew's Day, 1662.

Charles Haddon Spurgeon was surely one of God's choicest gifts to His church in Britain, and indeed throughout the world. We may well ask ourselves what lessons we may learn from his life and ministry. What is God teaching us through such a servant of His?

When Sir William Robertson Nicoll was asked what was the secret of Spurgeon's power he replied without hesitation, "The Holy Spirit." Here was a man laid hold of and filled with the Holy Spirit, and thereby made a fitting and effective instrument of the Holy Spirit. He was "a vessel unto honour, sanctified and meet for the Master's use, and prepared unto every good work" (2 Tim 2:21). From the day of his conversion as a lad of sixteen, until the day of his death, he had a single eye to the glory of God. Only one thing mattered to him, that he should do the will of God. And so he lived out his life for Christ, every minute of it. Earnestness in spiritual things and urgency in the service of the Lord were outstanding characteristics with him. He lived for God, in the pulpit, in the study, in the home, in the street, in the college, and in the orphanage. He calls us back to seek *first-hand* knowledge and dealings with our Maker and Savior. Much of present-day religion seems to be second-hand at the best. There is a lack of reality, of earnestness, of intensity. Men talk of God, but do not seem to walk closely with Him. Spurgeon did. There was a transparent sincerity about him, and an attractive simplicity, that proclaimed him to be a true man of God. We need to get back to the place of true fellowship with God, loving, abiding in Christ, constant dependence upon the Holy Spirit. We must be more often, and more receptive, at the Throne of Grace. We need to recapture the sense of the Sovereignty of God, and the primary importance of things eternal and spiritual. These are surely matters of which "he, being dead, yet speaketh."

Spurgeon calls us back, also, to sound biblical doctrine. Today there is a vastly different theological climate in the churches generally than in his day. Some of it is for the better; there is not the rancor between the denominations as once there was. But much of it alas, is for the worse. The Scriptures are no longer regarded as the divinely inspired and infallible Word of God, the rule of faith and conduct. The demythologizing, existentialist, anti-supernatural schools have had a devastating effect on the Christian outlook and emphasis of very many. Teaching on the death of Christ is far removed from the biblical doctrine of a substitutionary atonement for sin. The reformed doctrine of justification by faith alone is denied or passed over. Theology, in many quarters, is "Incarnational," finding its center in the fact of our Lord's identification with the human race, instead of His atoning work for fallen, guilty sinners. The notion is widely proclaimed that by the Incarnation God has united the race to Himself. But this is not the teaching of Scripture. The evolutionary theories of man have largely ousted the idea of the human race as fallen, under divine wrath, and needing redemption. Very rampant today are theories about the Being of God, the Person and Work of Christ, the destiny of man, moral principles, and the Church of Christ, which are utterly at variance with Scripture truth. Spurgeon would have us return to first principles, rooted in Bible doctrines. He would have no tolerance for the heresies of men like Dr. John Robinson, assistant-bishop of Woolwich, who would even reduce God to man.

A modern writer, Mr. Peter Howard, has this to say about the Church today:

> We are in the midst of a deliberate and global attempt to secularize society. I am a churchman. But I say with regret and shame that some churchmen today use their positions and the pulpits to join the secularization of modern man. These preachers are so determined to popularize Christ that they rob Christianity of the Cross. They put Christ down to man-size and worship Almighty man instead of Almighty God. Secularizers of society are Satanizers of society.

I fear that this is a true statement of many today in all denominations. Spurgeon said much the same thing in the "Down Grade" controversy. He would call us back to a Christ-centered theology and to the doctrine of the Cross as the only hope for a sin-sick world.

Further, Spurgeon surely calls us back to the Bible, and urges us to build our thinking and our lives on divine revelation, not on man-made theories. In God's Word, he would say to us, God has revealed absolute truth, and a firm foundation for our soul's salvation and our Christian life. All the problems of the mind of man, he would tell us, are adequately answered by the Word of God; and divine light from His Word falls on all human situations and conditions to illumine and transform. "The Word is truth"—build on it, he would urge upon us. "To the law and to the testimony; if they speak not according to this word, it is because there is no light in them."

He bids us return to expository preaching of the Bible. Too often today, where a text is taken, the sermon largely consists of the preacher's own ideas concerning it. Spurgeon's preaching was an opening up and an application of the Scripture facts and truths themselves. If we would but let the Word of God speak from our pulpits, we should be truly feeding the hungry souls of men, and making them see the light divine. Spurgeon himself, perhaps unfortunately, would never preach a series of sermons on connected Bible themes. He felt that this precluded the guidance of the Spirit from week to week. But today there is a great need for the systematic exposition of the different books of the Bible. People do not know what is in the Bible, or what the mind of God is on many subjects. The systematic exposition week by week of John's Gospel, of the Epistle to the Romans, or First Corinthians would be excellent for the establishing of believers in the faith. It is being done most fruitfully in some places.

Another great lesson from Spurgeon is his passion for souls. He aimed at conversions as well as the building up of believers, and God gave them to him in abundance. He saw clearly that men were either saved or lost. They were "in Christ," or under the wrath of God. Heaven or hell loomed before them, and there might be only a step between a soul and its immortal destiny. This outlook has been largely lost today, but man has not changed, nor the necessity for his regeneration. Nor is Christ any less able to save to the uttermost all who come unto God by Him. In many places Universalism prevails. We need to get back to the divine message, "Ye must be born again.... He that hath the Son hath life, and he that hath not the Son of God hath not life, but the wrath of God abideth on him." The Puritans insisted on bringing home to their hearers the guilt and power of sin, and the sufficiency of divine grace to overcome it. So did Spurgeon. He pressed home in almost every sermon the necessity of a work of grace in the soul to bring forgiveness, cleansing, and eternal life. We need to get back to the Bible view of things here also. The Church has no message at all for the world if it is not thoroughly Evangelical, calling sinners to the Savior.

Spurgeon would strongly oppose the various social "gospels" being preached so earnestly today, the pulpits that are sounding forth notions on housing, full employment, sex, crime, social security, and the like. He was not unconcerned with these things himself, but he knew his pulpit was not built to extol such things. He did not talk of social reform—he built an orphanage! Full salvation, and eternal security, he would remind us, are the only fitting topics for the New Testament pulpit.

Above all, Spurgeon would have us preach Christ—Christ only, and all the time. Christ was the glorious theme of all his sermons. Christ in His divine Person, and His atoning work, in the graces of His character, and in the effectiveness of His offices as Prophet, Priest, and King. Spurgeon, as he himself once said, found his way sooner or later to Christ from whatever part of the Bible gave him his text. The Bunyan-like simplicity and beauty of his speech set forth Christ lovingly and persuasively, and the result was that hearts were warmed, melted, and constrained to Him.

Spurgeon, if he lived today, would surely rejoice in the faithful evangelical ministry of Dr. Billy Graham, although he might not care for all the methods employed in his campaigns. He would not like "calls to decision believing that too much emphasis was being placed on the human will and not enough on the power of God, and the necessity of a thoroughgoing work of regeneration by the Holy Spirit. He would most probably desire to hear more of "calls to repentance" in modern-style evangelism. But still, he would rejoice that Christ and His atoning blood and saving grace were preached by Dr. Graham, and he would take his place at his side.

He would rejoice, too, in the wonderful opportunity that radio and television give for preaching the Gospel and declaring the truth of God, and no doubt if he lived today would avail himself of these media of communication. What would he think of the Ecumenical Movement? He would surely insist on the necessity of union on the basis of Scriptural truth. He would view with misgiving and alarm the efforts being made to bring about the union of churches while, at the same time, questions of vital doctrinal difference are ignored or belittled. And he would have no use for those who strove for a unity that includes the unreformed Church of Rome. It might well be that Spurgeon, if he lived today, would lead a movement of real spiritual unity amongst believers, based on The Evangelical Alliance, which was ever dear to him. He was never a denominationalist in the usual sense of that term; he believed that born-again folk were already united in heart and spirit and in devotion to the Redeemer, and if he were here he might well implement this thought in a new and comprehensive body of believers in fundamental Scriptural faith.

Dr. Hugh Martin, in his excellent book, *Puritanism and Richard Baxter*—a most valuable introduction to the Puritans and their principles, says:

> The Puritan seems a long way from us today, but there is more than one reason for considering again what he stands for. Bunyan's Pilgrim, "clothed in rags," with a burden of sin on his back and a Bible in his hand, is in strange contrast to the modern man. Yet, perhaps to recover belief in the reality of sin and of a divine revelation, and to have one's feet set upon a Way with a Guide, is something which we need, and which the men of 300 years ago might help us to recover.

Spurgeon, heir of the Puritans, has an imperishable example and message for us. Let us read Spurgeon again and consider his emphasis and the reasons for God using him so mightily and for so long for the blessing and salvation of hundreds of thousands of precious souls.

But let Charles Haddon Spurgeon have the last word:

> What then must that grace be that produces such blessed transformations? The wonderful phenomena of ravens turned to doves, and lions into lambs, the marvelous transformations of moral character which the minister of Christ rejoices to see wrought by the Gospel, these are our witnesses, and they are unanswerable.

> If we have the Spirit of God amongst us, and conversions are constantly being wrought, the Holy Spirit is thus fulfilling His advocacy, and refuting all accusers. If the Spirit works in your own mind, it will always be to you the best evidence of the Gospel. I meet sometimes one piece of infidelity, and then another; for there are new doubts and fresh infidelities spawned every hour, and unstable men expect us to read all the books they choose to produce. But we have fought most of their suggested battles over and over again in the secret chamber of our meditation, and have conquered. For we *have been in personal contact with God*. We have felt the power of the Holy Spirit over our soul; we have been stirred to agony under a sense of sin, and we have been lifted to ecstasy of delight by faith in the righteousness of Christ. We find that in the little world within our soul the Lord Jesus manifests Himself so that we know Him. There is a potency about the doctrines we have learned which could not belong to lies, for the truths which we believe we have tested in actual experience.

> The only person who can with saving power convince the world is the

Advocate whom the Father has sent in the name of Jesus. When He reveals a man's sin and the sure result of it, the unbeliever takes to his knees. When He takes away the scales and sets forth the crucified Redeemer and the merit of the precious blood, all carnal reasonings are nailed to the Cross. One blow of real conviction of sin will stagger the most obstinate unbeliever, and afterwards, if his unbelief return, The Holy Ghost's consolations will soon comfort it out of him. Therefore, as at the first so say I at the last, all this depends upon the Holy Spirit, and upon Him let us wait in the name of Jesus, beseeching Him to manifest His power among us.

Books For Further Reading

Quoting Spurgeon. This volume not only contains a Spurgeon bibliography but also more than 500 of Spurgeon's quotations, which have been arranged topically. Edited by Anthony Ruspantini and published by Baker Book House.

SPURGEON'S SERMONS

The New Park Street Pulpit. Sermons from 1855 to 1860, and published by Banner of Truth and Baker Book House.

The Metropolitan Tabernacle Pulpit. Sermons from 1861 to 1892, and published by Pilgrim Publications of Pasadena, Texas. Sermons from 1880 to 1890 published by Banner of Truth.

12 Sermons, Series. Each of the volumes in this series contains twelve sermons on selected topics. This series is published by Baker Book House.

Christ's Words from the Cross. A collection of Spurgeon's messages on the seven words of the cross which is published by Baker Book House.

Miracles and Parables of Our Lord. A three-volume work of Spurgeon's which sermons on the parables and miracles of Christ. Published by Baker Book House.

My Sermon Notes. More than 250 outlines prepared from some of Spurgeon's sermons, covering much of the Bible. Published by Baker Book House.

SPURGEON'S WRITINGS

The Sword and the Trowel. All Spurgeon wrote therein from 1865 to 1892. Published by Pilgrim Publications of Pasadena, Texas.

All of Grace. An earnest word with those who are seeking salvation.

An All-Round Ministry. Addresses given to the ministers and students at the Pastors' College. Published by the Banner of Truth Trust.

Chæque Book on the Bank of Heaven. Precious promises arranged for daily use.

Commenting and Commentaries. Republished in 1969 by the Banner of Truth Trust, with a Complete Textual Index to all Spurgeon's sermons.

Feathers for Arrows. Illustrations for preachers and teachers.

Grace Triumphant. A series of unpublished sermons printed after his death.

John Ploughman's Pictures and *John Ploughman's Talk.* Plain advise and plain talk for plain people.

Lectures to My Students. Three volumes of advice on the work of the ministry.

Morning by Morning and *Evening by Evening.* Devotional readings with which to begin and end the day.

Speeches at Home and Abroad. Discourses on various topics.

The Clue to the Maze. The so-called "honest doubt" of the New Theology answered by Spurgeon with "honest faith."

The Greatest Fight in the World. Addresses on the Down Grade Movement.

The Gospel of the Kingdom. Spurgeon's last work, on the Gospel of Matthew.

The Saint and His Saviour. Spurgeon's first book.

The Salt Cellars. Two volumes of collected Proverbs.

The Soul Winner. "How to lead sinners to the Saviour."

The Treasury of David. This seven-volume commentary is recognized as one of the finest works on Psalms ever produced.

Spurgeon on the Psalms. A faithful condensation of *The Treasury of David* by David Otis Fuller. This volume includes quotations from various expositors.

Trumpet Calls to Christian Energy. To arouse Christians to labor for Christ.

The Best of Spurgeon. A collection of select works of Spurgeon, which present his message and diversity of interest. Published by Baker Book House.

BIOGRAPHY AND HISTORY

C. H. Spurgeon's Autobiography. A four-volume work published in 1897. This was compiled by Spurgeon's wife and his secretary Rev. J. W. Harrald. Reissued as *C. H. Spurgeon: The Early Years, 1834-1860* and *The Full Harvest, 1861-1892.* A condensation into two volumes, edited by Iain Murray and published by the Banner of Truth Trust.

The Prince of Preachers. Written by James Douglas.

C. H. Spurgeon. Written by W. Y. Fullerton. (1920)

The Forgotten Spurgeon. An incisive, historical, and theological insight by Iain Murray. Published by Banner of Truth Trust.

The Genius of Puritanism, by Peter Lewis. Published by Carey Publications in England, 1977.

The Puritans: Their Origins and Successors. Addresses by D. M. Lloyd-Jones and published by The Banner of Truth Trust, Edinburgh. (1987)

From the Usher's Desk to the Tabernacle Pulpit and *From the Pulpit to the Palm Branch.* Written by Robert Shindler. (1892)

A History of Spurgeon's Tabernacle, Searchlight on Spurgeon, A Pictorial Biography of C. H. Spurgeon, and *A Traveller's Guide to Spurgeon Country.* Written by Rev. Eric W. Hayden and published by Pilgrim Publications of Pasadena, Texas.

Spurgeon: A New Biography. This volume, written Arnold Dallimore, is an excellent introduction to those who have never heard of the great preacher. Published by Banner of Truth Trust and Moody Press.

Evangelicalism in Modern Britain: A History from the 1730s to the 1980s. Written by David Bebbington and published by Baker Book House, Grand Rapids. (1989)

ATTENTION!!!

THE FOLLOWING BIOGRAPHIES ARE ALSO AVAILABLE FROM CHRISTIAN LIBERTY PRESS:

- Martin Luther: The Great Reformer
- The Mayflower Pilgrims
- George Washington: The Christian
- Robert E. Lee: The Christian
- The Life of Stonewall Jackson
- The Life of J. E. B. Stuart
- The Story of the Wright Brothers and Their Sister

TO OBTAIN A FREE CATALOG THAT DESCRIBES THE FULL LINE OF EDUCATIONAL MATERIALS FROM CHRISTIAN LIBERTY PRESS, PLEASE CONTACT:

Christian Liberty Press
502 W. Euclid Avenue
Arlington Heights, Illinois 60004
(847) 259-4444

Index